I could have been anybody,
therefore I am everybody
e.l.j.s.r.

100
EMPOWERMENT
Tips for everyday living

Dr. Edward Lee Johnson Sr.

ARCHWAY
PUBLISHING

Archway Publishing books may be ordered through booksellers or by contacting:

Archway Publishing
1663 Liberty Drive
Bloomington, IN 47403
www.archwaypublishing.com
844-669-3957

Scripture quotations are from the Holy Bible, King James Version (Authorized Version). First published in 1611. Quoted from the KJV Classic Reference Bible, Copyright © 1983 by The Zondervan Corporation.

ISBN: 978-1-6657-3438-7 (sc)
ISBN: 978-1-6657-3439-4 (e)

Library of Congress Control Number: 2022922370

Print information available on the last page.

Archway Publishing rev. date: 1/19/2023

The "Contemporary" Proverbs
by Dr. Edward Lee Johnson Sr.

your official handbook for conflict resolution

These 100 tips are where liberals, conservatives, people of all ethnicities and religions unite. They share a common goal of love, peace, freedom, self-reliance, integrity, hard work and discipline in order to galvanize humanity for the common good of all.

It takes immense pressure to produce a diamond, if you cave in under it; you are nothing more than gravel

Dr. Johnson's contemporary proverbs may be compared to King Solomon's book of Proverbs written in the King James Bible

- King Solomon's book of Proverbs, 15,000
- Dr. Johnson Contemporary Proverbs, 30,000

This book is dedicated to YOU!

If just "1" of my quotes helps you, an associate, or a loved one, it would be worth the price on the cover. If none of my quotes help you, you can return the book for a full refund.

Good relationships require growth, and you cannot properly grow without good information. If you are willing to make the necessary changes that are required to grow, these principles will guarantee you a more fulfilled life. "… people change only when they hurt enough that they have to, learn enough that they want to, or receive enough that they are able to."

You really don't know people until you know them, and you can only get to know them if they are totally transparent and you have spent a significant amount of time in their presence in order to know their ways. People who alienate themselves from others are actually trying to protect their weaknesses. Strong, confident individuals don't have these boundaries. It's the veil of human pride that is the most vulnerable, you can choose your direction but you cannot choose the outcome.

This life-skill handbook should be kept close by at all times as a reference guide to some of the challenges you are sure to encounter from day to day. Enjoy your journey through One Hundred Life Skills and Tips in the school of wisdom.

If a man is worth saving, he
will not drown. In this book I will teach
you how to avoid the trap of becoming a
public success and a private failure. No one likes
being told when they are wrong, but only an unwise,
simple, prideful, and/or foolish person rejects being
corrected when they are.

So, you think you are wise?
— Well, here's your test!

A wise man sees with his heart and not his eyes. If too much wealth is placed in the hands of an unlearned man, it makes him prideful. Too much wealth given to an educated man may eventually make him a tyrant. But if too much wealth is placed in the hands of a wise man, he will share it with the world. The world cannot generate enough wealth to satisfy a bad system and corrupt hearts. Standing shoulder-to-shoulder and back-to-front, you can put the entire world's population (nearly 7 billion) within the borders of Jacksonville, Florida, with space left over. The problem with the world is not the lack of resources to feed, clothe, and house everyone, because the world has the materials needed to sustain twice its current population. Our problem is the lack of vision, compassion, discipline, and leadership. When unrestrained by unnecessary bureaucracy, but properly led instead, the creativity, ingenuity, and gifting within the human spirit will rise to the challenge and overcome what may seem to be insurmountable odds. The real world is run and controlled by policymakers, wealth builders, and individuals with influence. Position yourself to be a changemaker if you intend to impact society.

Introduction

These relational tips are written to be used in the workplace, the churches, and the home, as well as during recreation and vacation time where you are likely to meet lots of strangers. Activists, athletes, entertainers, emperors, prime ministers, rulers, civic and political officials, farmers, world leaders, corporate executives, white & blue collar professionals, doctors, lawyers, nurses, husbands, wives, children, kings, queens, preachers, popes, priests, monks, gurus, sheiks, imams, rabbis, presidents, actors, butlers, bakers, candle-stick makers, and even "YOU" can prosper from the tips herein. Over the many years of my life it has become increasingly clearer to me that the greatest need in the world today is for there to be better relationships among humanity as a whole. Possessing the skills to communicate effectively is the key to establishing great relationships. My principles help you to rise above the fray of pettiness in order to accomplish your dreams with relative ease.

In my travels across the country and in foreign nations as well, I have discovered that people look, act, and sound different, but their innate characteristics are basically the same. The reason why astrological signs are so popular is because they expound on the human experience. Everyone who follow these signs are reading the same things. The twelve signs of the zodiac are supposed to tell you about your likes, dislikes, mate, special qualities, and even how you feel; just think about that for a minute. There are nearly seven billion people in the world, and only 365 days in a year. Within the 365 days, all seven billion people will celebrate a birthday.

Within the twelve months of the year, you can read from the zodiac signs, which would tell you something about the nearly seven billion people on Earth. If we were so uniquely different, it would be impossible to read and relate to seven billion people with such limited information. The signs of the zodiac are nothing more than the documentation of the human qualities as a whole and have absolutely no ability to direct you to any new revelation or success in life. The fact that the information was gathered from ancient history should further validate my point; we are all basically the same emotionally and intellectually. Our differences have to do with our ideologies and cultural background. If you took a person from one ethnic group and raised him within the culture of another, i.e. Whites, Blacks, Asians, or Hispanics, he would generally do what is most dominant within those cultures. Even when it comes to human biology, a person's color and features generally takes on that ethnic group after three or four generations of continuous breeding.

I purposely stayed away from any cultural issues in this book for the most part, because culture is basically the only difference we share within the human experience. Having said that, I would like to offer you some strong recommendations as to how to view your fellow man, and in doing so, I can promise you with a hundred percent certainty that this book will not only change the way you relate to other people; it will also change you. If you know deep down inside that some of what you struggle with daily has to do with your relationship with others—even your parents, siblings, spouse, and children—you may want to make this book a part of your library.

1

Make it your business to learn something about the culture of other people; it's the only difference between you.

Aside from your gender, culture, age, weight, complexion, physical and intellectual make-up, human beings are all the same. Other than trying to decipher it by my name, you would not know my skin color nor ethnicity by just reading this book. However, you can identify with the principles because they resonate as good human qualities. God's creative genius established the human race in the earth.

Humanity began with a family, which God intended to become the model by which all other families would be patterned thereafter. However, when the first specimen was corrupted as a result of disobedience, the corruption trickled down to all. The differences that we share as human beings aside from physical appearances have only to do with the way we "think." Because of our limited knowledge of man's structure, we have placed the emphasis on the outward appearance, which has absolutely nothing to do with the real person on the inside.

Man is a spirit, and the spirit lives in a body; but the two are totally different in purpose. A fish lives in water, but water is not a fish, and a fish is not water. Your spirit lives in a body, but your body is not your spirit. Once we completely understand the commonality of the human race, we can better relate one to another based on God's original plan for mankind. If you begin to practice the principles, your relationship with your fellow man will be better. The same evil spirit that corrupted the first man and woman wants desperately to corrupt you as well.

2
People don't follow you because you are great; they follow you because of what you do for them.

The basic instinct of human beings is self-preservation; they will flock wherever or to whomever to satify their desires. It took me years to come to terms with the fickle nature of some people. We all find ourselves at one point or another looking for fulfillment from others. What we don't get emotionally and spiritually from parents, we seek through friends and associates. So when people associate themselves with a particular person or group, it's primarily because they are looking for some type of fulfillment: spiritually, financially, emotionally, socially, etc. Never become overconfident in what you offer them thinking they are with you for you, because it's not about you necessarily, but what you do for them. One of the toughest lessons I had to learn in life was this empowerment tip. Having watched people come in and out of my life over the years has taught me never to think that what I do in life is about me. I suffered emotional pain on many occasions because I generally give all of my heart when I'm attempting to build relationships; that's not always the case with the other person. However, I was no longer able to meet their needs, so they cut ties. Never get hung up on your ability, just serve humanity out of a heart of love. People in general will seek you out as long as you can produce for them, the moment you cannot perform, they will defect to the one that can. And this should be okay with you. People have a right to decide who they want to establish a relationship with.

3 Never take advantage of another person even if you think you can get away with it.

Your character defines the real you. It has been said that the best way to really know a person's character is to find out what he will do if no one is watching. Whereas your personality is what you project to the public, character is who you really are in the dark. It really takes someone with good character traits to refuse the opportunity to mistreat, abuse or deceive someone else. The human heart has always been a nesting ground for deceit, and this is why it is so important for good morals to be instilled within the formative years of life. We have numerous narratives throughout the Bible, which is the book that defines moral character, where people did heinous things to one another. Cain killed his brother Abel thinking that he had gotten away with it only to be cursed by God and condemned to wander the earth for the rest of his life. He became a pariah and had to flee for his life simply because he was vulnerable to the deceit of the heart. Jacob, in another Bible story found in the book of Genesis, took advantage of his brother by taking away his birthright in exchange for a cup of pottage. However, he had to run for his life once his brother found out what he had parted with for so little in return. In this life, your treatment of others will eventually come back to you in one form or another. It is known as the law of sowing and reaping. The way you treat others is directly correlated to your relationship to God.

4

If you are going to assume something, just let it remain an assumption and never a conclusion; you could be wrong.

This may be a bit amusing, but I cannot count the times that I have accused one or more of my six children of moving something of mine from a place that I was absolutely sure I placed it, only to find the object where I left it sometime later. It is always hard to go back and say I found it, so I usually don't mention it again unless they ask me. I believe that things like this happen sometimes just to remind us of our own shortcomings. I am sure if you think for a moment or two, you will remember a similar incident in your life. Never come to a conclusion based only on an assumption. There are thousands of people locked behind bars and many others who have been put to death over an assumption. Thank God for DNA testing that has helped a lot of inmates regain their freedom. Many friendships are broken, and family relationships destroyed simply because a conclusion was drawn from an assumption. When we are in the middle of a quandary, it is easy to point the finger because it gives us a sense of closure. If you are going to make an assumption, assume that you could be wrong in your assessment of the situation. In this case, you sould probably be more sensitive to the individual about whom you have made the assumption. Never conclude until you have sufficient evidence: it's the law.

Dr. Edward Lee Johnson Sr.

5

Develop a sense of humor, it is life's shock absorber.

A wise man once said, "laughter does good like a medicine." This is true primarily because much of our physical health is directly tied to our emotional well-being. It is obvious that God has a sense of humor because He has designed laughter to be of such positive benefit. I don't believe that ministers of the gospel are called to be comedians, but they should have a sense of humor. We should never take ourselves too seriously; none of us will get out of this world alive. The Bible even speaks of having our mourning turned into laughter. Rebecca laughed when the angel predicted she would have a child in her old age. Then, when it came to pass, she named the child Isaac (which means "laughter"). Children developed cancer far less than adults because they are more carefree about life. They don't generally carry the burden of working a stressful job, paying bills, and navigating through life from day to day. Jesus left this empowerment tip on record over two thousand years ago: "Take no thought for your life, what ye shall eat, or what ye shall drink; nor yet for your body, what ye shall put on." I am not suggesting that people with a sense of humor do not develop cancer; I would say that people who have a great sense of humor are more prone to get through things faster, live longer and happier lives. It would even help if you laughed at some of your own mistakes; it would be equivalent to opening a pressure release valve. I often hear my dad (a preacher) who in ninety-nine years old make the following statement. "Don't take life so serious, you are not going to get out of it alive." Laughing at ourselves and humorous people can sometimes be our greatest relief.

6 There will come a time when you will have to cut ties, but make absolutely sure it is the right time.

People who are genuine about their relationship with other people take no pleasure in cutting ties. However, it is imperative to do so at times, but make absolutely sure it is the right time. We often use the term "follow your heart." I am not sure this does not mean follow your feelings. I use the phrase "follow your feelings," because I have noticed over the years how easy it is for people to cut ties with one another solely based on feelings. However, don't be in such a hurry to sever the relationship; maybe the other party just needs time to think, or, you could be wrong. Sometimes I find myself on the wrong side of an issue as I am trying to build relationships with others. I may feel as if I'm reaching out too much and that there is no effort from the other party to reciprocate. I have even gone to drastic lengths to delete all contact information; not because I do not want to pursue the relationship, but because I begin to feel vulnerable in the situation. However, I find myself recovering the information in order to reach out one more time. I know when it is right to move on only if I have heard from God on the issue, but even then the door remains open. You cannot violate another person's will, and it does not matter how much you may want the relationship, it has to be in the will of the other party as well.

Dr. Edward Lee Johnson Sr.

7

The talent you possess is a gift to others; don't act as if it's yours.

Nothing that we learn or accumulate in this life belongs to us; it is a gift from the Creator. If we think of our gifts, talents, and accomplishments as if they belong to us, it makes us selfish, shallow, stingy, greedy and arrogant. The Giver of all good gifts may allow you to share in some of life's good things; you should become a conduit and freely share those blessings. Generosity is a condition of the heart. You should see yourself as no more deserving than any other person in the world even if you have gained much. The time will come when you have to return everything that has been entrusted to you, and give account for your stewardship. This could become a very painful transition for you if you acted as though it all belonged to you. If you have the talent to create things, sing, teach, play sports, and lead people etc., do it all with grace and appreciation for the One who afforded you the gift. If you have a healthy attitude toward the Giver of the gift, you would know that God gave it to you in order for you to help other people. Of course, you should enjoy what you do and the fruit of your labor; however, you should be liberal with all that you possess, knowing that it is temporarily on loan to you. People who are truly free and generous in their gifts and talents will bring pleasure to others as well as themselves. And even more importantly, your Creator will take pleasure in you.

8 Why does the topic of race still dominate our discussions in America after nearly 400 years?

Blacks, Whites, Hispanics and Asians in the United States, for the most part, share the same schools, worship facilities, residential communities, clothing, laws, doctors, lawyers, modes of travel, recreational facilities, cuisine, and language. So how is it that we still claim to be of different races? There is no rational or logical sense to the topic of race in America other than our ignorance of what the term race really means. What we call race, especially in the United States, is simply a cultural divide that is driven by ideology. As a result of the diffusion of many cultures, we have literally become the "American (Race) Culture." Race in antiquity had nothing to do with color, because race was defined as a group of individuals who shared the same culture. The argument that we have some physical differences won't pass scrutiny because homogeneous people in some places of Africa, China, India and northern Europe certainly don't see eye to eye on all things. Just examine the turmoil that exists among people of the same make-up. There is absolutely no monolithic community on Earth where everyone acts and thinks just alike. Our physical appearance or biological DNA is not what defines us as humans. Human beings are spirits, and spirits do not have a color. Ignorant, bigoted individuals and special interest groups exploit this topic. The problem of humanity is not skin, but sin. And by the way, there is only one race; it's called the "Human Race."

Dr. Edward Lee Johnson Sr.

9

The greatest relief from stress rarely comes from anything you do externally.

Exercise and stress relief programs are a multi-billion-dollar industry, and yet the most inexpensive program to relieve stress, is ignored. The most prolific writer in the New Testament states that "bodily exercise profits little." As I am writing this book, there is a study all over the news suggesting that exercise may have very little to do with curtailing weight loss or improving health issues. Excess weight and stress go hand and hand, and you cannot eat away stress. If and when an individual ever comes to terms with his or her emotional and mental state and resolves the issue there, stress would subside considerably. Overtaxing ourselves mentally, and emotionally and our inability to let go of personal frustrations is the driving force behind stress. If you take advantage of the 100 principles in this book and develop a healthier attitude toward others and yourself, I can guarantee you a less stressful life. Begin to feel great about yourself inwardly and not just set out to become a great achiever. Your greatest weapon against stress is the way you think. Once you have affirmed yourself to yourself, things can change. When you have a positive mental and spiritual attitude, it relieves stress from the mind just like a filter traps debris. The human spirit was designed to be happy and free. Unresolved issues over a period of time create stress. Deal with the issues first, and watch the progress.

10

If you think the other person is wrong, chances are he or she feels the same way about you.

If I ask you to think of the times that you have debated with a person because you thought he or she was wrong about something, you would probably lose count. This is primarily true because there are always three sides to every story: yours, theirs and the right side. So the next time you find yourself in a debate about an issue, even if you think you are right, allow the other person the chance to be right as well. Anytime you begin to argue and get angry to get your point across, it is an act of selfishness. To handle yourself, use your head, but to handle others, use your heart. If you use your heart and take care in dealing with your opposer, you may be able to convince the other person that you are right. I can disagree or debate with a person on any subject imaginable and still not get angry with the person. I think it's a skill that was gifted to me. The one huge debate in our culture today is the subject of homosexuality, endorsed by the president. I think it is wrong, but I can hold a conversation with a gay person and even hug him. I may be hospitalized and a gay doctor could be responsible for saving my life. It's not the person I have the problem with, but the principle for which he stands. However, every individual has a right to his opinion, and you cannot force him to see things your way. Sometimes the best thing you can do to solve a problem is to leave the person alone because the problem may be you.

11

Smile often—it is the photo of your heart.

A smile is the single most defusing factor when you meet an individual for the first time. It is tantamount to a breath of fresh air or the bright sunshine. According to doctors, and these figures will vary, we use four muscles to smile and sixty-four to frown--this is sixteen times as many. Try practicing your smile in the mirror; it's not vanity. As a kingdom citizen, you represent the highest order on Earth; it's the principles of your heavenly Father. So often Christian people portray such a gloomy disposition in the public sphere trying to look pious, and yet we expect the world to believe we have all the answers. Everyone will not hear our message. However, we should not be the cause of them rejecting it by the way we approach them. Sometimes the first impression you leave with a person is the lasting one. Everyone is attracted to a smile; even if it's a fake smile, it will attract you. However, I do not suggest that you fake a smile unless it's all you have for the moment. A smile is transmittable--if you do it, in most cases the other person will return the courtesy. As with laughter, which is nothing more than a full-blown smile, it helps your immune system and assists in maintaining good health. Lee Mildon, a great personality, says, "People seldom notice old clothes if you wear a big smile." Think of a smile this way, it's a gift that you can give to everyone, and it will not cost you a dime.

12 There is no force that is more powerful than the indomitable human spirit.

History is replete with stories of groups and individuals who decided to win against what seemed to be insurmountable odds. Nelson Mandella, the former president of South Africa, spent 29 years in jail because he was an activist who wanted to see his people free from the unjust laws of apartheid. The American Negroes who were rooted up from their Mother Land of Africa endured 150 years of the most inhumane treatment in history, only to rise out of the ashes of shame to become doctors, lawyers, professional athletes, and superstar entertainers because of the will of the human spirit. No other ethnic group on a broader scale in history suffered such direct onslaught. There is a young man that was born in Australia by the name of Nicholas James Vujicic. As a result of a rare disease, he was born with no hands or legs. Growing up he struggled immensely as he came to terms with his condition. However, as a teenager, he found faith in God and has become one of the most sought-after ministers of the gospel and motivational speakers around the world today. I have actually watched him on Christian television as he preached to thousands. He is married, he swims and is literally unfettered by life's challenges, all because he has the will to make something out of his life. The will to fight and win against adversity is a gift from the Creator; He never created a loser.

13

If you must tell a lie, don't; therein "lies" your character.

Telling untruths is an age-old character flaw that has been practiced from the inception of humanity. This concept was introduced to man by the archenemy of God, Satan. Jesus declared that Satan was the father of all lies. "He was a murderer from the beginning, and abode not in the truth, because there is no truth in him. When he speaks a lie, he speaks of his own: for he is a liar, and the father of it." The express purpose of a lie is to deceive. Deception is the very reason humanity is suffering at all levels. Murder, rape, theft, corruption, adultery, greed, and more, all are birthed out of a lie. When I was a child the elders would say, "Once you tell one lie, you have to continue to lie to cover the first lie." A person who habitually tells an untruth for the sake of committing an evil act is under the influence of Satan. There is a difference between just telling the untruth and being a liar. Abraham told an untruth, but he was not a liar. It is tantamount to cancer and cancer cells. Cancer cells, which we all have in our bodies, in themselves are not harmful until they become numerous and attach themselves to one another. When this happens, it destroys vital organs. Telling lies habitually in order to deceive is not the same as telling an untruth in order to divert an evil act, such as the actions of Abraham in the book of Genesis, and Rahab the harlot in the book of Joshua.

14 Always look the other person in the eyes when you are having a private conversation.

The eye is the window of the soul. When you face a person and look him in the eyes while talking, even if you are being dishonest, which I do not suggest, you will become more convincing. I am not suggesting a stare-down contest, but frequent eye contact will connect you with the other party. There are generally two reasons why a person will not face another when talking; either he is intimidated and insecure about himself, or he is lying. As a person of character, you would not want either of these impressions to be believed of you. Good moral characteristics give you the fortitude to face any man without fear and intimidation. People who are pure in their heart can sometimes convince those with bad motives to polish up their acts and become better individuals. As a believer in God, it is incumbent upon you to convince others of your walk in life. We have been called to be witnesses of the most important message in life; it is about the life of God's Son. You have to be convincing enough to win over those individuals who are unbelievers and skeptical about your purpose in life. Eye contact is one of the cardinal rules of public speaking. See yourself as representing the greatest cause ever, your speech should be full of grace, yet piercing as an arrow. Let your words be seasoned with grace and they will penetrate the hearts of men. Never become aggressive but always be assertive when you speak.

Dr. Edward Lee Johnson Sr.

15

If a person tells you that you offended him, ask for his forgiveness even if you did not intend to hurt him.

The words "I'm sorry," and "I love you," are two of the hardest for some people to utter. People do not like to say "I'm sorry," because they do not want to suggest they were wrong. They refuse to say "I love you" because they do not have a strong sense of generosity. With some men, to say "I love you" makes them feel soft or insecure in their manhood. These words can head off relationship and emotional damages that can sometimes last for a lifetime. If it were you being hurt by someone else, would you not want the same courtesy? I would go one step further and say, if you feel that you have offended someone, you should go to that person and ask for forgiveness even if he or she has not confronted you. It is only our ego, pride and the feeling of self-importance that will keep us from genuinely saying I'm sorry. There were times when I was made aware of things that I did that offended a person even months and years later; I was ready and willing to say I was sorry for the misunderstanding the moment it was brought to my attention. To say you were wrong is not an act of weakness, but the opposite is true. People who are strong in character and have a good feeling about who they are should find it easy to apologize if necessary. Love and kindness are the fundamental principles of a true Christian character. You are an ambassador of the King, represent Him well.

16

Outward accomplishments are simply the manifestation of an inward vision.

Every successful accomplishment derives from a carefully thought out plan: it's the pursuit of VISION. Do you have a vision for your life? If yes, find a trusted mentor who can give you the advice that you will need in order to fulfill your goals. God places mentors in our lives that can steer us in a positive direction. A vision is usually developed over time as a result of some trials and error. You need to have a vision in life because it's your blueprint for life's accomplishments. If you don't know where you are going, you will not know when you get there. When your vision is clear, frustrations are at a minimum; growing pains are the only problem you will face. Visionary leaders release their vision into the hearts of those who are loyal to the cause, and from their vision come productive factories, churches, medical practices, engineering firms, sports teams, and every other producing entity in the world. Helen Keller moved the world because she had vision even though she did not have sight. Write your vision and make it plain so others can follow. People will always rally behind a visionary because it helps them to get in touch with their creative genius as well. It has been said that everything started from nothing, but that's not the truth; there has to be a visionary. Everything that exists in this world is a result of the ultimate visionary, God. In the beginning He spoke the creation into existence.

Dr. Edward Lee Johnson Sr.

17

God's kingdom cannot be established as long as our culture, pride and social status stand in the way.

If you must disagree, let it be on principle and not the person. In essence, you don't have to be rude, obnoxious, and offensive to disagree with an individual. The greatest problems dividing our public discourses would be solved in a day if everyone simply knew how to publicly disagree without the mudslinging. The tenor in our political arena suggests that you can say anything even if it's a lie, just as long as you can get away with it. I have witnessed numerous relationships destroyed because of individuals who did not know how to handle their differences. There is a stark difference between disagreeing and becoming disagreeable. Mature people who disagree understand and respect the right of the other person to have his own opinion about the issue. People who are weak, immature and self-seeking will allow a disagreement to turn into dislike, resentment, anger and eventually hatred. When emotion reaches this stage, an individual becomes very uncomfortable in the presence of the other. A person who cannot be reasoned with is called irrational. These condescending and dissenting behavioral patterns are the reason there is so much unrest in the public sphere. Those who possess the spirit of God are called peacemakers. The Kingdom of God will be established when the peacemakers inherit the Earth. In judging your own actions concerning disagreements, would you say that you are a peacemaker? Military and public safety officers keep the peace, but you were chosen to be a peacemaker.

18 There is a friend that sticks closer than a brother, but that's only as long as you are friends.

I have associates and friends that I probably interact with more than many of my siblings, but, I hold the relationship with my biological brothers very dearly. There are some friends that are closer than brothers, but not in every case. Sibling rivalry is an age-old struggle that started with the first two known brothers in the world, Cain and Abel. Esau and Jacob struggled in the womb and became bitter rivals in their lifetime. Joseph's brothers threw him in a pit and sold him into slavery. Abimelech, one of Gideon's sons, killed 70 of his brothers. The Bible is replete with tragedies that existed among brothers. However, I believe if they all had the opportunity to do things the right way the second time around, they would see it differently. When friendship is broken, a brother may be all you have left. As a pastor, I have watched people who have come to the end of this life, and the only person that stood by them as they transitioned from life into death was a member of the family. The family is the foundation of every civil society, and that is why Satan works overtime to destroy the family bond. No matter what happens between parents and siblings, your primary goal in life should be to keep the family bond strong. I do know that some people are impossible to reason with; just don't let it be you.

Dr. Edward Lee Johnson Sr.

19

Be sensitive to the feelings of others.

People in general are sometimes not as logical as they are psychological. The latter has more to do with the way we feel rather than the way we think. Essentially, our thinking is driven by the way we are feeling about ourselves or about a particular issue. To state it more succinctly, we see things as "we are" and not as "they are." A person who is irrational is almost always emotionally unstable. I sometimes find myself apologizing to my wife because she is quite sensitive to some of my words. This is not to suggest anything derogatory about her or anyone who is prone to sensitivity. As humans, we are the products of our associations and environment. Someone who is not so sensitive will never be able to totally understand someone who is, and vice versa. Being sensitive to a sensitive person simply means that you will not trivialize what he or she is feeling by pretending it does not exist. There is an ancient African proverb that says, "Never judge a man until you have walked a mile in his shoes." Two school teachers got into an argument because one accused the other of not helping her to retrieve the children's lunch as it was falling from the table. Moments later, the offended teacher discovered that she was delusional due to a dizzy spell and the children's lunch never fell to the ground. She quickly apologized for her attitude, and they remained close friends. Our perception is our reality.

20 The family is the fundamental building block of society and of a happy, productive life.

If your family life is in order, chances are everything else in life will fall into place. There is no question in my mind as to who the most important people in the world are to me. They are my wife, children, parents, siblings, then friends and associates. I grew up in a home where the sense of family meant everything. My parents celebrated nearly sixty years of marriage before my mother went home to be with the Lord in February, 2005. The values I hold dearly and the happiness I share with loved ones and friends can all be attributed to what was instilled in me as a child. My love for God, parents, siblings, my elders, friends, associates, respect for authority and tolerance with those who don't agree with me were all lessons I learned at home. It is imperative that those of us who believe in the Biblical foundation of marriage begin to give our children a well-rounded view of all people, and an even a more tolerant view of those who don't share our values. What children are taught in the home by parents generally seals their fate for life. Right will always win in the end, and when you know you are right on an issue, you don't get in a railing fight with those who don't believe like you do. We are taught not to be overcome with evil but to overcome evil with good. It is not our job to change the minds of those who disagree with us, but to tell the truth in love and allow God to deal with the hearts of those who don't agree.

21 Being right should not be your primary goal, but being heard; if a person will hear you, maybe you can convince him or her that you are right.

Sometimes we can become so obsessed with being right that we become wrong in doing so. Anytime you set out to make your point, you must understand that people do not have to listen to what you have to say. Even if you are their boss or superior, they can choose to quit before they listen. When you set out to make your point, even though you may be right, it has to be done in a way that will compel the other person to listen to your point of view. We may have the right answer but the wrong attitude. Always keep your composure and make others feel as if they matter in the equation. People may forget what you say, but they will not forget the way they felt in your presence. The way you speak and the words you speak will usually determine if you are being heard. Life and death are in the power of the tongue, and the words you speak may determine the destiny of the hearer. As a believer in Christ, you are in the people business, don't ever forget this. Secular institutions are in the business to make money in most cases, but the believer in Christ has been called by God to speak wisdom to the world on His behalf. If you are not careful to win others over with kindness, you may never get them to hear your message of reconciliation. And don't ever forget that some people are born for adversity; you cannot pay them to come in agreement with you, so move on to those who will.

22

The only power you have over the future is yourself; start there and change the world.

What do Abraham, Moses, and Christ have in common with Martin Luther Jr., Abraham Lincoln and Martin Luther King? They were all men, and their stand in life changed the world. Every major turn of events in world history was spawned by one man. If you have big dreams and want to change the world, you have to change first. World changers are those who see the world, not as it is, but the way they want it to be. You have to become the person you want others to be. From there, spend the remainder of your life impacting, persuading, coercing, preaching, teaching, and doing everything else in your power to solicit converts. it's just that simple. We speak what we know, but we actually reproduce what we are. I'm not saying that if you set out to change the world, you can, but this is the way it's done. I would further say that it is vain and foolish for anyone to set out to change the world. Changing oneself should be your priority. However, if you simply live by your core conviction, and touch the hearts of enough people along the way, you might just change the world. Once you find the purpose for which you were born, live life to the fullest and are happy with your decisions, people will follow you, perhaps enough to change the world. Your future is actually now—don't wait for tomorrow to make the necessary changes in your life. Tomorrow was not promised, but today is your gift; it's your "present."

Dr. Edward Lee Johnson Sr.

23

Poverty has more to do with the lack of creativity than it does the lack of resources.

There is an ancient proverb that says, "Give a man a fish and he will eat for a day, but teach a man to fish and he will eat for life." The most empowering factors to the American ideology are freedom and creativity. Creativity is the ability to dream, and along with your dreams, resources will come. It is quite interesting to note that slavery, the death to creativity, could not stop the creativity of George Washington Carver, Lewis Latimer, Granville T. Woods, Elijah McCoy and a host of other black inventors who helped birth the industrial revolution in the United States. Creativity is a God-given gift that is uniquely woven within the human spirit that compels man to mimic his Creator. Man was designed and created to be self-governed and work in harmony with the universe. Prior to man's existence, perfection existed within God Himself. Extending Himself through the vessels of humanity was His pleasure. If you plan your work and work your plan, the resources will come in time. Successful people are successful because they are willing to do what unsuccessful people refuse to do. Poverty, ignorance, sickness, disease are all instruments of Satan that he uses to destroy the creative genius that is in you. Even those who do not acknowledge God are gifted with His creativity. Creativity comes out of a heart that is free to dream If more people are given a hand up, the freedom to dream, they wouldn't need a handout. If you think you can succeed, you will, if you don't think you can, you won't.

24

Always look for the good in other people, and even if there is no good in them, it would be good to know.

As a young man in my teens, I remember this fellow whose name was Frank. He was a notorious alcoholic and floundered from place to place. I don't know that he ever lived in a stable place of his own after becoming an adult. However, there was one thing that he could do well, and that was playing the harmonica. I thought to myself, "Wow, this guy is good for something!" Even the worst of individuals, who have made bad decisions in life, still have some good in them; good people sometimes do bad things. Some of the most talented people in the world are locked behind bars. I have learned never to judge a man by his weakness but by his strength. All of us are just one step away from a grave mistake. One mistake can sometimes cause you a lifetime of misery. I remember when I enlisted in the Armed Forces and was stationed at Fort Knox, in Kentucky. Some of my buddies and I were sitting around in the barracks just making small talk, eating popcorn and potato chips. I was very short-tempered at the time, and when one of the guys tried to pass a bag of popcorn to me, the fellow next to me snatched it before I could get my hands on it. I became so angry I pulled out a knife and tried to cut him—and could have actually committed manslaughter. Thank God for grace, because that could have landed me in jail for a long time. Always try to appeal to the good in people; it's the same grace you would want extended to you if you fell on hard times.

Dr. Edward Lee Johnson Sr.

25

Your relationships with God and other people are the keys to building His kingdom on Earth.

Every member of the Body of Christ should master great rela-tionships. However, in my opinion, the number one problem in the church today is bad relationships. This is precisely why I decided to write this book. I am in hopes of helping believers and nonbelievers better their relationships with one another. It is quite baffling to read the Bible and see how members of the Body of Christ should relate to one other, and then to compare how we actually treat fellow members of our spiri-tual family. Even the Bible itself is replete with bad examples of relationships. However, Christ left us a kingdom model of how to establish good relationships. One study says there are over 38,000 factions within Christianity. Do you believe that if Christ was here among the church community, He would be pleased with the way things are among the body of believers? Each of the more than 38,000 different groups seem to be more concerned about covering and controlling turf than it is about becoming one as Christ commanded His followers. If it is indeed our actual goal to follow the Lord in the estab-lishment of His kingdom, there has to be a new paradigm; the course we have taken will not get us to the kingdom. It is long overdue for true faith leaders to take another look at what actually exists between us currently versus what Christ and the Apostles left on record in the New Testament.

26 Getting to know people can only be done through relationships.

You can read books and study the traits of people, know about their likes and dislikes, and get a fairly good assessment of who they are; but if you expect for people to know you, some of your time must be invested in them. There is absolutely no substitute for personal interaction. Visibility and interaction is what makes the game of politics such an arduous task; and perhaps this is why many politicians don't want much to do with the public once getting into office. Some individuals love a crowd but cannot stand the people. High profile people such as politicians, preachers, actors, and entertainers who are on television have developed a bond with the viewers. As artificial as it may be, we do feel as if we know the individuals. If it is your intention to make an impact on the culture, you must be willing to develop meaningful relationships; and the television will not do it. As an ambassador of the kingdom of God, you should shun the crowd and go out of your way to connect with people. Take a personal interest in people and not just see them as a step to your next conquest. Always keep in mind that it is a privilege and honor to have influence with people. People in your life are blessings from God assigned to you in order for you to complete your kingdom assignment. Get to know these individuals and establish real, and not superficial, relationships in order to build the kingdom of God.

27

A leader is one who knows how to convince others to follow, even if they don't know where they are going.

Always follow the leader, but be sure the leader is taking you where you want to go. It is very unwise to connect with anyone until you have some sense of who they are. So often people will connect with others solely on an attraction, only to find out in a short period that it is not where they want to go. This happens most often because people have not really gotten in touch with who they are, so they try to find their identity in other people. Taking the time to find out God's purpose for your life is the most valuable lesson you can learn. Charisma is the ability to influence others, but it does not necessarily translate into character, so don't be deceived by charisma. A person can be ever so convincing but his motive may not always be pure. The late President Ronald Reagan made popular the phrase "Trust but verify." Always hold people accountable for their words. If an individual will not honor their own words, how can you trust him to honor yours? During the 1970s, a cult leader by the name of Jim Jones led nearly one thousand people to their deaths because he was a charismatic leader. Do not follow anyone blindly, especially preachers and politicians; get to know the person first. If you are fairly certain that his or her values are in alignment with godly character, perhaps this may be the place God has assigned you.

28 If you hate, you lose everything; if you love, you gain all things.

The most powerful word in the human language is love; and the most destructive is hate. To love and truly love is the ability to look beyond a person's shortcomings and faults and give to that person something that he or she does not deserve. Every deed that's ever been done by man will ultimately be judged by God and rewarded or condemned based on the principle of love. Even self-sacrifice on behalf of another is not always an act of love but self-aggrandizement. The Greek language gives us four basic words for love: agape (sacrificial and unconditional), eros (sexual), storge (natural affection), and philia (brotherly). 1 Corinthians 13 literally defines the kind of love that God honors, and all other love has to be defined through this prism. Jesus became the greatest example of love ever. God offered Him sacrificially on behalf of fallen humanity and Jesus willingly submitted to the will of the Father by rendering His life. Hatred from the ones that tormented, humiliated, and ultimately killed Him was the plan of Satan. Had Jesus succumbed to hatred of His enemy, He would have lost it all—and so would we—but He chose to love, and gained everything; so can we. If you love and love effectively, it can neutralize hate. True love never violates the will of another, unless the person is insane. If your life is pleasing to God, even your enemy will have to be at peace with you. Never give your opponent the advantage of making you jealous or hating him; he who hates loses the game.

Dr. Edward Lee Johnson Sr.

29

If you are hurt emotionally by someone, let the person know immediately and give him or her a chance to make it right.

Too often people who have been offended by other people will harbor resentment without the offender even knowing he or she gave insult. When I feel that I have been insulted, and if I cannot get over it, I will approach the other person as quickly as possible. What I have witnessed on many occasions is that when it happens to some people, they will tell a third or fourth party but will never inform the offending party of what he or she did. This type of behavior is childish. Perhaps it is not even childish because most children get over hurt quite rapidly although they have tantrums, and they are extremely playful. But adults, on the other hand, will hold on to issues to their graves. Jesus, the greatest peacemaker of all times, left a conflict resolver on record, but people rarely refer to it. Here is what He said, "If your brother offends you, go to him and him alone, and tell him his fault." As a pastor, I cannot count the times that I have had to lead individuals to this passage in order to assist them in resolving issues. Sometimes people will not listen even after they have read it. We generally go to other people first before confronting the individual in an attempt to resolve the issue because we want to be validated and find justification for our action. Or even worse, we use this as an opportunity to slander because we don't really want a resolution.

30 Republicans and Democrats are the epitome of the Sadducees and Pharisees; neither party loved Jesus.

The Sadducees and Pharisees boasted of their love for God, but both parties hated Jesus—go figure. If you vote with a blind loyalty for either political party in America, failing to see the flaws and the good in both, I seriously question your loyalty to Jesus as well. The two party system is the process by which our public officials in Washington chose to run the country. So, the mudslinging between the party members is nothing more than the pot calling the kettle black. If either party is corrupt, that simply means the country is corrupt because the parties represent what we have become as a nation. The two parties coming together (Congress) to make laws that the party members fight against is tantamount to parents producing a boy and a girl, and both parents calling their children bastards. It's insanity! Until politicians renounce party allegiance and begin to run the country like a body of mature adults, we will continue to have a house divided against itself. People will always choose sides when there is a fight. Democrats are in favor of gay marriage and abortion. Republicans are against both (so they say), but they sanction same-sex unions, and many of the party leaders don't fight to ban abortion once in office. Your civil rights allow you to pass property to anyone you choose in the form of a will and a trust, so why another law? Abortion is murder, and same-sex union is redefining marriage; God is against both.

Dr. Edward Lee Johnson Sr.

31

If you start an argument, finish it—not by arguing, but with a resolution.

You should never allow an argument to go unsettled if it is in your power to resolve it. In order to do this effectively, you must begin to consider the other party that is in the crossfire. Think in terms of what you would want if you were being attacked. If your ultimate goal is to be heard and not to be degrading, there is a way to do it. You can first begin by lowering your voice. My voice normally gets elevated slightly in a debate, but I never allow myself to get angry. However, this is not the case with many people. King Solomon left this wisdom tip in the scriptures: "A soft answer turns away wrath." Once your voice is lowered, continue to speak, and speak directly to the issue only. Don't drag into the conversation other issues that are not relevant to the topic of discussion. People who hold things in for a very long time have the tendency to dredge up old issues during a debate. Once you have made your point, give the other party the opportunity to respond. If the response is satisfactory to you, then the issue is resolved. If not, perhaps the two of you will need to solicit the help of a mutually respected arbiter who will assist you through the conflict. If the other party refuses the help of a mediator, he or she is not interested in a resolution, so leave him or her alone. Never argue with a fool; someone may hear you arguing and not know which one of you is the fool. Neither person may be a fool, so why behave like one?

32

God blesses you through people; treat them right or you may not have anyone to deliver your blessing the next time around.

People are your greatest resource. It does not matter how much material wealth you accumulate—it would not be worth anything if you did not have anyone to share it with. As a young boy, I listened to a preacher who frequently came on television on Sunday mornings. He would always close with these words: "Be nice to the people going up, because you may have to face the same people coming down." The blessing and favor that God grants to us generally comes to us through other people. Just begin to think for a moment as to how you arrive at the material things in life. It is either from employment or a gift. If you own a business, it is usually the people who work for you that do the bulk of the work. If a gift is passed on to you, it's probably because someone has found favor in you. If you have a job, someone else hired you. Loving people should be something that you work hard at perfecting if you intend to be a great leader. Of course, it's not easy with some people, but you have to know that hurt people hurt other people. Anyone who sets out to hurt another person through retaliation or spitefulness is generally acting out of their own hurt. You cannot go wrong as long as you have a heart to love people unconditionally; that's the heart of your heavenly Father. Always do right by others. It will come back to you in the form of a blessing, even if it doesn't come from the people you helped.

33

It is impossible for the Bible to be the book of men only.

I have been studying the Bible consistently for nearly 40 years, and have found it to be the source of all moral behavior on Earth. The Bible is the most profound book ever, simply because it's not just a book written by men, but a library revealed by God. It has been read by more people than any other book in the world. How do you explain narratives that span over four millennia, written by more than 40 contributors who knew little or nothing about the other, that nevertheless contain a seamless overarching message? The Bible is simply the guiding principles from God to man, teaching him how to find his way back to the Creator. Genesis 1& 2 are the account of creation. Chapter 3 tells the story of man's defection from his Creator. Chapters 4-6 record the corruption of humanity and God's promise of judgment. In Genesis 12, or roughly 2,000 years after the creation of Adam, God called Abram, who later became known as Abraham, to start the redemption process of humanity over. It was through Abraham that all the families on Earth would be blessed. From Genesis chapter 12 to Revelation 22 is one seamless story of how the restoration process of all mankind is possible. The story of the Bible is complex, and yet simple; you only have to provide faith to believe it. It is the faith that God gave to you, but must be activated through action; faith without works is dead.

34

The greatest lesson to be learned from an offense is to reward the offender.

One of the cardinal rules of Biblical Christianity is to forgive the person who has wronged you. Some people spend a lifetime trying to get even by retaliating, making more money, living in exclusive neighborhoods, disassociating from other people, hating and even killing in order to get even. To forgive is the single most liberating source in the human experience. Jesus gave His life in order to teach this principle. Harboring unforgiveness does more harm to the offended than it does the offender. To reward the offender is not to charge him with the offense, but to forgive him. Unforgiveness is directly linked to selfishness. This may sound a bit unfair but it's life's reality. Think of it this way, you did not choose to be born, and neither did you have any control over the way you were raised. However, the sovereign God of the universe decided to give you the gift of life. If you actually believe this, then you have to come to terms with the fact that He knew everything that would happen to you in this life. You are responsible for the decisions that you make, and you choose to forgive or hate. Your life is a gift from God to you, and what you do with it is your gift back to Him. Choose love and forgiveness, the greatest gifts. In the book of Job, chapter 42:10, God restored Job and gave him double when he forgave his friends. Always forgive your enemies, and only get even with the people who help you.

Dr. Edward Lee Johnson Sr.

35

Success is nothing more than a tenacious individual who refused to let failure become his or her legacy.

If you are successful in life, thank your enemy; it was probably he or she that motivated you to succeed. Aside from those who have had it handed to them, everyone who has achieved any reasonable amount of success has a story to tell. Success is the fruit of arduous toil, sleepless nights and the severing of ties with those you would have hoped to remain connected. Highly successful people are not those who go after success just for the sake of it; they are individuals who possess a drive that they themselves don't totally understand. However, they are able to see results before they achieve them, and that becomes the energy that drives them when others around them aren't driven at all. It goes back to the God-given creativity that I talked about in success tip #23. Abraham lied about his relationship with his wife, Sarah. Moses was a murderer before he became a deliverer. David was an adulterer before he was laid to rest as the greatest king in Israel's history. Abraham Lincoln suffered 10 major failures in life before becoming the president of the United States; but we know all of these men as successful people. Perhaps no one can tell you about pain before success like a woman who has given birth to a child. Only after holding the child will she tell you that it was worth it all; success is no different. "It's not how many times you fail, but that you never stop trying." And, it's not the size of the dog in the fight, but the size of the fight in the dog. Don't quit.

36

The best way to get your point across is by doing it, not saying it.

It has been said that a person with an experience is never at the mercy of a man with an argument. Monday morning quarterbacks are the guys with all the answers as to why the game was lost even though they never played the game. The take away is to never spend your time debating with someone who tries to tell you how to win a game that he does not know how to play, or, is not willing to play. Everyone is not going to believe in your dreams. We find the classic story in the book of Genesis of Joseph's brothers hating him because he was inspired with a dream. His brothers became jealous of him and tried to silence him by selling him into slavery. Jealous people are those individuals who don't like your dreams simply because they do not have one or are not sure of theirs. When you have become convinced about what God has assigned to your hands for a given season in your life, you must put blinders on and cultivate your rows until the crop begins to grow. Blinders are what you put on a mule to keep him from being distracted while pulling the plow. You must be patient with all men but don't lose any sleep over people who do not believe in you. It is impossible for everyone to believe in you; however, you must believe in you. Once you are convinced of your dreams, passionately pursue them and converts will come in time. People may question your motive but they cannot argue with success.

Dr. Edward Lee Johnson Sr.

37

A good leader is simply a follower who was next in line.

If you expect to become a good leader, you should learn how to follow. Being a good follower does not suggest that you are weak because you have to play second fiddle. It simply means that you are not over anxious to take on a task that has not been assigned to you. Even if you think you are ready, never fight your way to the top because you may have to fight your way back down. When God needed a replacement for Moses, He chose Joshua, who was Moses's administrative assistant. When Elijah was taken up to Heaven, Elisha got his mantle because he was close by his side. Paul mentored Timothy, who became a successful leader in the first century church. When you follow closely, you are at an advantage because you are able to sometimes see what the leader doesn't see close up. Work in harmony with the people God has partnered you with and when it's your time for an elevation, He will see to it that you are not passed over. Psalms 75:6 teaches us that promotion comes from God. People who are overly ambitious will generally cut corners and become deceitful just to move up the chain. If you can remember that God is your source of promotion and not man, even your enemy will be used to elevate you when it's your time. Never fight, mistreat and overlook other people in your aspirations to achieve. Always follow the leader closely, and when the mantle falls, it may fall on you. If it doesn't, God has a better plan, just continue to be patient.

38

The very person you ignore may be the one that God sent to you.

Pride is by far the most detrimental sin of all. Here is a direct Biblical quote: "These six things does the Lord hate: yea, seven are an abomination unto him: A proud look, a lying tongue, and hands that shed innocent blood, A heart that devises wicked imaginations, feet that are swift in running to evil, A false witness that speaks lies, and he that sows discord among brethren." Notice that the word pride is at the very top of the seven deadly sins. I really don't believe some people know when they are acting out of pride. Sin originated out of pride. I keep a close watch over myself, lest I become guilty of pride as well. It is a common practice of mine to be kind, gentle and accessible to anyone who requests my time. I do not have special people that I cater to. There are some people that warrant more of my time, such as my spouse, children, and those that I am mutually connected with for the kingdom, but I will make the time for anyone who genuinely needs me. Here's another great passage from the Bible which helps to make this point: "Be not forgetful to entertain strangers: for thereby some have entertained angels unawares." Don't ever forget that God sometimes uses drastic measures to get our attention. He used the burning bush to project His voice when speaking to Moses, an ass to speak to Balaam, a fish to swallow up the prophet Jonah and a cock to remind Peter of his denial of Jesus. Never ignore anyone that has requested your time; it may just be your test.

Dr. Edward Lee Johnson Sr.

39

If you know the entire Bible, you still will not know the Bible until you have the Spirit of the Author.

The Apostle Paul said it best when he coined the phrase, "The letter kills but the spirit gives life." This statement holds such profound truth simply because the letter of the Bible was actually drafted by individuals who were functioning under the influence of the Spirit of God. The Bible is history, but it is not just history. It is the revelation of God's universal plan for mankind. From the time that Christ left Earth, millions of people have died defending the Bible. However, Christ laid down His life so that we could have the Bible. Having a zeal to memorize and quote the Bible is not the same as possessing the gift of its transformation. Transformation can be understood more clearly through this illustration: If you took a sheet of paper and severed it into one thousand pieces, it would still be paper. If you took the same sheet of paper and burned it, it would be transformed to ash. Without the process of transformation, you will only have the information of the Bible. A computer with the ability to connect you to information from around the globe is of no use unless it is connected to a power source. The Holy Spirit is the power source of the Bible. When you are connected to this source, He reveals Himself to you. Wisdom, power, blessings, healing, forgiveness, faith, hope, and love will flow out of you when you have the spirit of the author of the Bible.

40

As a result of a nation's success, inflation is tantamount to a self-inflicted wound.

If the escalation of wages, goods and services were the same across the board and at every level, inflation would be a wash. On the other hand, when politicians, demagogues, bureaucrats, and people with much wealth and power collaborate to make laws that basically stifle the poor, it's an act of evil that will not go unpunished by God. According to Wikipedia, "a 2011 study by the CBO [Congressional Budget Office] found that the top earning 1 percent of households gained about 275% after federal taxes and income transfers over a period between 1979 and 2007. From 1992 to 2007 the top 400 earners in the U.S. saw their income increase by 392% and their average tax rate reduced by 37%. The share of total income in America going to the lower earning 80 percent of American households (also after federal taxes and income transfers) has dropped to less than 1/2 in 2007." The fact that nearly 50% of Americans do not pay federal income tax is not the problem, but that 50% of Americans are subjected to such income disparity and the laws permit it is the problem. And, what about sales, property and all the other taxes that are paid by those who don't pay income taxes? Those who make more should pay more. God instituted a 10% tax over 3500 years ago and it has not changed; if it worked for Him, why can't it work for us? If the government would better manage its income, it wouldn't need more taxes. Consequently, business would not be forced to increase cost on goods and services.

41

If you make a mistake, it may not be the end of the world; but it could be the end of a season in your life.

The story was told about a young, aspiring banker who was being mentored by a more experienced banker. The young banker asked the question: How did you become such a great banker? The experienced banker replied, "By making good decisions." The young banker asked, "How do you make good decisions?" "By making bad ones," said the mentor. The question is not whether or not we will make mistakes in life, but whether we learn from them. Some mistakes can be rectified, and life can go on as usual, and there are others that will become life-altering decisions. All things do work out for good to those who love God. All of the things that happen to us will not be good, but they can work together for good if we learn from them. Sometimes the worst thing that can happen to you is the best thing that could happen. People who are resilient and resolute know how to take a lemon and make lemonade. By all means reconcile with your past. If you have been hurt by a situation, or if you have hurt someone else, it does not have to be the end of the world, but you must learn from the mistake. The experience could very well be a turning point for you, but it should motivate you to be a better person. Before you were born, the creator knew precisely what would take place in your life. He also knew that He placed faith in you, extending you the ability to rise above every challenge. Faith only works when you work it. Faith without works is dead.

42

Have you heard it said, "Don't hate the player, hate the game"? But if the game is foul, so is the player.

This wisdom tip is colloquial or street language that is used by people who are usually involved in nefarious activities, something that you would want to stay as far away from as possible. According to another old saying, "Don't lie with a dog because you may get up with fleas." In essence, you must learn how to choose your friends carefully. Everybody who seeks to connect with you may not have your best interest at heart. You will do yourself a great service to explore the background of an individual before committing to friendship. Always watch your enemies carefully, and your friends more carefully. More often friends can hurt you the most because they are closer to you. I borrowed the following quote from the Apostle Paul: "Be not deceived, evil companionship corrupts good morals." If you want to be known as a person with good character, you cannot have close associations with people who are known to be corrupt. However, even a corrupt person should know that you are accessible should he or she need your help making a change in life. There are hundreds of people that I will not hang out with, but there is no one that I would not assist if I knew it would change the individual for the better. You may be the only lifeline left, so never close the door on an opportunity to help. However, if you know that a person is involved in foul activities, hate the game and the actions of the player, but never the individual.

Dr. Edward Lee Johnson Sr.

43

The role of the Preacher is the greatest office on Earth.

The role of the clergy is to prepare humanity for eternity; the role of kings, presidents, monarchs, and other civic leaders is to manage the temporal affairs of a nation. A grave mistake on the part of politicians may cause the country to go to war, but a pastor's mistake may determine if you spend eternity in heaven or hell. Now which of the two would you say is the most important role? I have traveled to several foreign countries and many places throughout the Unites States, and sightseeing is one of my favorite pastimes. My love and passion for ministry have formed a special place in my heart for pastors. When I travel, I love to visit churches. Having been called to the ministry as a teenager and having a father as a pastor as well, I know the seriousness of this role. It is clear to me that God has placed an awesome responsibility upon the shoulders of pastors. We are not simply called to pacify people and just play the role as good men in the community at the church; we have been assigned by God as the vanguard of the Faith. This is the Faith that is founded upon an immutable and irrefutable truth that will stand for eternity; there is no higher calling on earth. If you are a pastor or a member of the clergy, my challenge to you is to make sure you do not see yourself as a grasshopper. Read the story in Numbers, chapter 13:26-33 and it will help you see why I use that term. We are of the royal spiritual lineage of Abraham, Moses, and Christ.

44

People may disagree with you, but they will generally respect you if you respect them.

Every civil human being wants to be respected. However, not everyone knows how or is willing to give the same in return. We are told in many cases that respect has to be earned; I totally disagree with that logic. Respect simply means to consider the humanity of other people, and to treat them the way you would prefer to be treated. Personally, I will respect a dog as long as he does not come into my yard and try to bite me; should that happen, I may be forced to kill him. You should always be the first to be courteous and polite to everyone you meet. Allow the other people to act discourteous if that's their choice, but never stoop to their level in such a case. Neither should you have such a high opinion of yourself that would make you think that others are beneath you. If you consider yourself to be great, then you are obligated by God to humble yourself in order to reach the least of humanity. Sometimes people may mistake your confidence for arrogance, and when they do, you are obligated to show them that you are not. Be kind and considerate in all that you do. As a citizen of God's kingdom, you should be the first to master the art of diplomacy. You can catch more flies with honey than you can with vinegar. Be nice and kind to everyone you meet, and in most cases, the kindness will be reciprocated. There are some rude, obnoxious, arrogant, self-serving and unbearable people in the world, just don't let it be you.

Dr. Edward Lee Johnson Sr.

45

A good leader is one who carries the load on his shoulders, but a great leader is one who shares the load with others.

Why do the work of ten men when you can put ten men to work? Some people are so hands-on they refuse to delegate. It is truly a great thing when one person can get a task done if dependable help will not show up. I've had to wear several hats for a great portion of my life, as most great leaders do. At this stage in my life, I am now able to shift some of my attention to other areas because God has sent the much needed help. I am such a perfectionist, I will have to be absolutely sure you are just as good or better than I am at a task before I will solicit your help to do it for me. However, I have learned that true greatness is the ability to see greatness in other people, and great leaders are never threatened by the abilities of others, but solicit their help in order to accomplish desired goals. When you are secure within yourself about your God-given assignment in life, you don't worry about others taking that away because no one can be you better than you. If you are not sure of who you are before delegating power to other people, jealousy and suspicion will consume you. Study the life of King Saul and David in the book of 1st Samuel in your Bible. When you are great and truly great, you are also graceful. Graceful people inspire others to achieve greatness as well. All great leaders are also willing to take their share of the credit, and blame, if the task fails.

46

Faith without works is dead, and work without faith is a burden.

One of the most alarming statistics that I have seen is the rate at which pastors are dropping out of the ministry. Twenty years ago, I read my first article concerning the negative effects of the ministry upon pastors. James Flynn, Director of the Ministry Program at Regent University, writes, "It's interesting what standing in front of people can do to you week-by-week when you have regular preaching responsibilities. If you don't watch out, the Bible can become nothing more than a text for your next sermon. Your relationship with God can be reduced to sessions of begging, pleading, and bargaining for something for next Sunday morning. Such is the life and weekly grind of the preacher. That weekly grind can take its toll and claim you as its next victim if you don't watch yourself" (www.re-newaldynamics.com). If you are a member of the clergy, it is imperative that you approach this profession from a faith-filled and God-called commitment. Ministry is stressful enough, and without the absolute commitment of faith in the God of the work, and the work, it could be a death sentence. Pastors are dying young at an alarming rate alongside other highly stressed professionals in the corporate world. Christ died to lift our burdens and not to overwhelm us with them, so this problem is not because of Christ, but our lack of faith in Christ to do His work through us. God's presence comes to guide us; not drive us. He lifts burdens, not overwhelm us with them.

Dr. Edward Lee Johnson Sr.

47

It's okay to be No. 1 as long as you understand that No. 1 means you are at the bottom; the only number that is less than 1 is 0.

What Dr. Martin Luther King Jr. called the drum major instinct, the desire to be out front, is perhaps the greatest detriment to world peace. The human ego is at the forefront of every human deviance. Some of humanity, if not most, has been yearning for world peace for thousands of years. Each passing generation looks for a charismatic leader who would lead them in that direction only to be disappointed once this figure is positioned into power. This is true primarily because it is the innate desire of human beings to be out front for their benefit and not yours, whenever that position is threatened, drastic measures are taken to maintain the #1 spot: Satan in Heaven, the Pharaoh of Egypt at the birth of Moses, King Herod during the time of Jesus, and Adolf Hitler in modern times are just a few individuals that come to mind. Jesus taught His disciples that it was ungodly to strive for the number one spot. He taught His disciples paradoxically that the real number one person in His kingdom is really the one at the bottom. He literally personified and demonstrated this principle by girding Himself with a towel and washing the feet of His disciples, a task that was reserved for servants. This is something that would be beneath the #1 individual. So, if you really want to be #1, just know it automatically puts you at the bottom. The greatest in the kingdom of God is the least among men.

48

Never give up on a task unless you are thoroughly convinced it's time to quit, not when others say so.

True leaders have a strong resolve and are tenacious in their pursuits. When you have been inspired to accomplish a task, you go to bed with it on your mind, and when you arise it's still there. If you quit before you are totally satisfied with your results, you will never be fulfilled for wondering what could have been. If you have to give up on a task once it has begun, there should be something from that experience that has prepared you for the next task in life. I purchased a small AM radio station in 1991 and kept it for 9 years. I struggled financially for the entire 9 years with some really memorable times during my ownership. I had hopes of upgrading the signal because it was hard to reach my target audience operating at 880 watts. The signal was transmitting about 15 miles from the area that I really wanted to reach. I was able to move the studio into the right area but I could not get the FCC to grant me the license to upgrade the wattage. After about 8 years into my radio career, two stations came into the market with the same format that I had, with the intention of siphoning my audience. They were successful, and at this point I was completely satisfied that I had given my best, so after 9 years in the radio business I sold the station. Without any regrets, that experience has prepared me for what I am currently doing in my life.

Dr. Edward Lee Johnson Sr.

49

Never agree with a person if you really don't agree.

It is better that you never develop a relationship with an individual than to establish one that is not mutually beneficial. Every relationship you develop should have a positive impact on all of the parties involved; it is the spiritual law of reciprocity. God has so ordered that we should be helpers one of another. There are some people who really believe that you have been put here to serve them, and their only goal is to use you. If you ever find yourself on the giving end and never receiving from a relationship, something is wrong. If you do not know who you are, someone else will define you. Proverbs 18:13 says, "It is shameful and foolish to give the answer before hearing the question." Before you ever agree to anything, you should have a good understanding of the terms. You would not get on a bus to travel without knowing its destination. Neither will you agree to work a job and not know the wages, or precisely what the job entails. Many marriages and other relationships are severed every day because someone said they agreed but they really did not. How can two walk together unless they are in agreement? The answer is simple; either one or both parties are being deceptive. If you don't agree, make that position clear upfront. You will be respected more if you are decisive about your feelings and decisions.

50

A college degree is not worth the paper it is written on if it does not translate into everyday life.

The economic downturn in our nation has brought the value of a college degree under great scrutiny. Much of the inflated tuition cost is the result of corrupt people at the top taking more money than they need and frankly, don't deserve. Nearly two-thirds of the graduates with a four-year degree have no success in obtaining employment in the field they actually studied. (see Forbes.com) In spite of these facts, tuitions have continued to skyrocket, and student loans are defaulting at alarming rates. For the past twenty years, we have watched many of our industries shift overseas and numerous IT jobs created by college dropouts. I will be the first to tell you to pursue additional knowledge by whatever means necessary, but do not over burden yourselves with massive amounts of debt in a college education if you have not focused on what the degree will actually do for you. I believe that a two year technical degree with a whole lot of "mother wit" (common sense) is worth more than four years without a goal. Learning has more to do with practical, hands-on experience than just the ability to memorize the answers to a test. As a teenager I learned the value of hard work from my father. In elementary school I picked up soda bottles by the carton, put them on my bike that I personally patched together, and rode two miles on a dirt road just to make a few dollars. In today's world, you have to come to the table of negotiation with more than a piece of paper; you have to prove you can produce.

51

A global vision is not worth anything until it has been proven locally.

Think globally but act locally, should be the disposition of a great leader. If you cannot master where you are, how will your plan work anywhere else? From the time of the Tower of Babel, people have had grandiose visions of conquering and ruling the world, but they cannot manage what is in their own house. God is currently shifting the atmosphere within the financial markets, churches and in government. We have witnessed the economic collapse and the overthrow of governments in the Middle East and parts of Europe. The leaders of our nations are drunk with power and there seems to be no soundness at the top anywhere. This is happening simply because human nature, which is out of touch with God, does not understand boundaries. Every effort of a man becomes nothing more than a power grab and self-serving if the human heart is not conditioned to serve other people on behalf of God. When a man serves on His behalf, he must serve humanity based on godly principles. "He that rules over men must be just." Sometimes leaders become preoccupied with a vision to reach around the globe, but they haven't built healthy relationships with the people that are nearest to them personally or geographically. The light that shines the farthest distance shines the brightest at home. Reach out to your city, and let your city reach out to the world with you.

52

Doing things for people will not necessarily make them love you; but developing a relationship with them will.

One of the greatest mistakes that you can make in life is to try and buy a person's loyalty. You may buy the loyalty but it would not be to you, but to the money. My life experience has taught me that no amount of material things will make a person devoted to you. This is precisely why millionaires and billionaires suffer from the same problems that poor people do when it comes to relationships. You have probably seen on television or read in the tabloids of how some children of rich people treat their parents. Sometimes they will even go to drastic means to have them killed just to inherit their wealth. There is absolutely no substitute for building godly trust and loyalty in relationships; you must touch the heart of people. When a true bond has been developed, loyalty becomes as natural as breathing. Humans are relational beings, and when a relationship is not at the forefront, we use people and things to fill the void. Always make it your aim to develop a rapport with people whom you are closely associated with. Money and material things are temporal, but relationships are for life. In case you haven't noticed, the book in its totality is devoted to relationship building. It is the absence of strong bonds that causes the destruction of families, communities and nations.

53

True generosity must extend beyond what you give monetarily.

The story is told of the chicken and the pig on their way to church discussing what they were going to give in the offering once they arrived. The chicken readily said, "Well I am going to give two dozen eggs for my offering today." The pig responded, "For you to give those eggs as an offering is not a problem, but for me it's a sacrifice because I will have to give a portion of my hind-parts." True generosity has more to do with giving with a genuine desire to have your heart touch the hearts of the recipients; if your gifts are not from the heart, it's vanity. Some people give money just to try and make their guilt over having excessive possessions go away. Some parents will spend large sums of money to do things for their children, sending them to elaborate places but will not sacrifice their time to establish strong bonds and healthy relationships. Entrepreneurs will sometimes give money to impoverished neighborhoods, but they wouldn't dare to step foot in the community to grace the people. Politicians will readily give out ear-marked tax dollars to their favorite pet project, but when you look at what they gave from their personal income, you really get to see just how generous they are. Much of what some people call generosity has nothing to do with the people they give to, but the desire to be "seen" as a person who is generous.

54

A leader knows what to do because he has done it, or knows someone who has, and made it work.

The phrase "never let a blind man sell you glasses" is sarcasm suggesting that since he cannot see, he can't help you. However, even a blind man can teach you a thing or two if he himself has mastered the technique. Would you say that Helen Keller, a 20th century blind and deaf activist who made an indelible impression in the American culture, can teach you something from her life? What about Stevie Wonder, a musical genius who was born blind and is one of America's leading entertainers. Can you learn from him? Great leaders are not necessarily great lecturers, but they have mastered a craft and can show others how as well, because they have done it. When great leaders don't know what to do, they know who to call in order to find out what to do. No man knows it all, and every man has a king and a servant in his bloodline. Never be afraid to say you don't know, but always be prepared to teach others what you do know. Now the man who you should not allow to sell you glasses is the one who has no vision; you can have sight but no vision. A vision comes from within and sight comes from the outside. Leaders are true visionaries who can see the future and lead you to a place of success. He is one who has placed his desires to succeed over all other personal ambitions. "He who knows not and knows not he knows not he is a fool, shun him. He who knows and knows that he knows is wise, follow him." (Confucius)

Dr. Edward Lee Johnson Sr.

55

A poet can tell you how to find success, but a teacher will show you how.

Have you ever heard of a "talking head"? They are people who have all the answers but cannot solve the problem. Some radio talk show hosts, politicians and even some preachers have mastered the art of speaking; in street terms they have the "gift of gab." However, when it comes down to putting the word into practice, too many of the talking heads are not willing to spend the time to teach you skills; they are too busy cornering the market for themselves. That is why there are some preachers who can preach but not pastor. Real teachers are uniquely gifted individuals that give to you what is in their hearts for free, because it's who they are. It reminds me of a passage that was spoken by Jesus, "The scribes and the Pharisees teach with Moses' authority. So be careful to do everything they tell you. But don't follow their example, because they don't practice what they preach." (Matthew 23:2) Poets are interested in arousing your emotions; teachers are interested in empowering you intellectually. A poet will keep you coming back to hear what he or she has to say; but a teacher equips and sends you out to teach others as well. A poet tells you how to memorize, but a teacher explains the process of how to master your goals. A poet may give you a fish, but a teacher teaches you how to fish. Choose a trusted mentor any day over a talking head who is only interested in keeping you listening to what he or she has to say. Now, if he is a poet and a teacher, that's a good thing.

56

Isn't it ironic that the greatest leader who ever lived never led anyone anywhere?

Very few of the seven billion people of the world's population who know anything about Jesus will dispute the fact that He is the greatest leader Who ever lived; and yet, He never led anyone anywhere. He spent the entire three and a half years of what we know of his public life in the New Testament mentoring about a dozen men who had little or no social status with the Roman or Jewish elites. We only know of Him traveling less than 100 miles away from His home while on Earth. However, what He did manage to accomplish was teaching people the art of personal responsibility. Man was created to be self-governed; and to look for a leader to do for you what you are personally responsible to do for yourself is irresponsibility. Politicians, religious leaders and teachers should all have one goal in mind, and that is to teach people how to manage their own affairs. A true leader must Master his personal affairs, teach others how to do the same, and then develop a team of leaders who will become equally responsible to one another for the good of all. Anyone who asks you to follow him without these three goals in mind is not looking out for your best interest, but his own. A godly leader will not exalt himself above people, which is what many politicians or a demagogue does. Becomes a servant unto them on God's behalf. All true leaders lead by influence and not control; people who are obsessed with control are actually weak.

57

The greatest proof of your love for God is defined by the way you treat other people.

"I love God, but I cannot stand those church people." So often I see people who act completely out of character to the Christian faith, and yet they are the ones who preach the Bible the most. This is not a statement of judgment but discernment, because I do understand we are all a work in progress. One of the most recent and blatant examples of bad behavior portrayed by Christians was when members of the Westboro Baptist Church of Topeka, Kansas picketed the funerals of military veterans. This behavior was un-Christian; nothing can be found anywhere in the Bible to justify it. When Jesus was approached by the religious leaders who dredged up the adulterous affair of a young woman, they wanted to test Him on His commitment to the law of Moses. When Jesus openly pardoned the woman and rebuked the leaders for their hypocrisy, their conscience condemned them and they walked away. A more appropriate behavior on the part of Westboro Baptists would have been to assist the family members by helping them through the grieving process. Who knows the number of individuals that could have come to Christ as a result of the kindness that should have been shown to them. It is through His love and kindness that God uses to draw men. To disagree with an individual's sexual preference is one thing, but to boycott a funeral and offend grieving family members is wicked.

58

Life is a game and money is the score; this concept is great so long as you understand that life is only a game of monopoly.

I have only played the game of monopoly once or twice in my life. I do vividly remember when I played for the very first time and, after the game was over, thinking, this game is a great life lesson. You actually go through the game racking up properties and taking in the dollars only to give it all back at the end of the game. How ironic is this? Life is played exactly the same way. Every passing generation produces its classes of poor people, millionaires, billionaires and multi-billionaires. These highly successful individuals purchase for themselves mansions, airplanes, yachts, islands and even people. At the end of the game of life, everything has to be turned in and reissued to the next set of players. The only difference between the two games is that the "life game" has consequences. "But God said unto him, you fool, this night your soul shall be required of you: then whose shall those things be, which you have prepared." (Luke 12:20) Jesus spoke this parable about the rich man who had put all his trust in his wealth. If your perspective on money is based upon scripture, you will not have to concern yourselves with the consequences of eternal damnation. However, if the only score that you keep in the game of life is money and your relationship with God is neglected, not only will you lose the money, but you will lose your soul as well.

Dr. Edward Lee Johnson Sr.

59

If you are going to trust a person with your inner-most secrets, trust him or her to be human as well.

If you have a secret that you don't want anyone to know, don't trust it to a confidant who promises not to tell. Every human has a limit to which he or she can be trusted; the ultimate secret is the one you keep to yourself. Unless you are absolutely certain that it would be okay if your secret eventually gets out, keep it to yourself. Once you have shared it, it may not remain a secret. The best thing you can do with a delicate situation in your life is to settle it in your heart with God. Once it has been settled there, even if someone does know, it will be okay. Harboring unsettled past mistakes is a miserable feeling, and can cause illness in your body, take years off of your life and even cause death. We all want to think that we have someone we can trust with issues that trouble us. And for the most part, there is that person we can trust our heart with; but trust him or her to be human as well, because individuals with the best intentions may let us down. The worst pain can sometimes help us to grow; as you grow within yourself, it should not matter too much what people think of the mistakes you have made. As long as you have rectified your mistakes and made things right with the parties involved, leave the result up to God. True friends don't care about your mistakes, and your enemy doesn't believe in you, so why spend time worrying about what your enemy thinks?

60

Being critical is sometimes necessary, but never be critical without an appropriate solution to help.

The above quote is a lesson that I learned in elementary school. I can vividly hear these words coming from my teacher. I do not remember if it was something related to what was happening in the class (one of those teachable moments) or if it was just one of those life lessons. I have tried to live by this rule because it speaks to the character of the individual. If you are criticizing people just for the sake of being critical, this is an act of evil. In my assessment of other people, I always consider myself as well because all of us have some weak areas in our lives. Perhaps you never meant to be critical just for the sake of it, but now you know better; and when you know better you will do better. If you have ever had someone to do it to you, then you know how ugly and degrading it feels. Remember the golden rule which says, "Do unto others as you would that they do to you." Perhaps you can even handle criticism, but is this something you would want done to you? I try very hard to make sure when I have to discipline my children in any way that I give them some valuable instructions as well, so they can learn from their mistakes. Children eventually become adults and they will usually pass on to their children what was taught to them. The world will be a much better place when we try to see life through the eyes of other people. If you are willing to pitch in and help the individual you are being critical of, that is a good trait to possess.

Dr. Edward Lee Johnson Sr.

61

The human will is the composite of knowledge, energy and motivation.

These are God-given traits that come from within and only the individual can control his or her will. If a person chooses not to cooperate, do not violate his will by forcing him to submit; he will resent you. One of the things that I deal with on a weekly basis is counseling married couples, which I enjoy immensely. It is one of my greatest delights in ministry because I enjoy seeing people happy, especially couples. The relationship of husbands and wives has been likened to that of Christ and the Church, and should be one of love, harmony and affection. When I begin to counsel the couples that come before me, my first question to the couple is: do the two of you want this relationship? If either party says no, or is unsure, I will end the discussion of the relationship and begin to deal with them individually. If one party is not sure if he or she is willing to stay in the relationship, there are no grounds for a discussion. It has to be an act of the will to enter in and stay in a relationship. Harmony in any type of relationship has to be an act of free will. God Himself will not violate the human will, and that is why we are free moral beings. Adam and Eve made a choice to violate the covenant that God established with them. Because the covenant had to be agreed upon by Adam and God, God severed His initial covenant with Adam because of Adam's disobedience. Two parties must be equally willing to develop a relationship.

62

Your greatest gift in life is your relationship with Christ.

There is literally nothing that you can do in this life that is more important than developing a relationship with God through His Son. When I speak of a relationship, I do not mean joining a church and participating in religious activities. Participating in church does not mean you have a relationship with God any more than having a ring on your finger means you will not cheat on your spouse. A relationship with God entails obedience, faith and loyalty to the plans He has set forth for you to obey. Jesus made it clear that to call Him Lord and not obey His word is to deceive oneself. God's original plan was that humanity should have an eternal, harmonious relationship with Him. The plan was breached, according to Genesis 2 & 3. From that point in human history, God extended grace (a second chance) to man in order to reestablish the broken relationship. God spoke prophetically in Genesis 3:15, to start the process of salvation, and made it official in Genesis chapter 12:1-3 by calling a man by the name of Abram to establish the covenant. Through the lineage of Abraham, 430 years later, Moses brought the laws of the covenant, and roughly 1400 years later God sent His Son, Christ, to complete the process. If you take the time to learn and obey the words of God's son, your relationship with God will be restored. It is the most wonderful experience that one can have in a lifetime. If you haven't, give Him a try.

Dr. Edward Lee Johnson Sr.

63 The B.I.B.L.E.

There is no book like the **Bible;** it is the bestselling book in all of history. The **Bible** is the story of man's relationship with his God, written by man but revealed by God. The **Bible** contains the superior word of God revealed to man with instruction on how to relate to God and our fellowman. The gift of the **Bible** is inspirational and supernatural in that its content would be impossible without God. The very heart of the **Bible** is Christ; without Christ the **Bible** would be just another history book. What makes Christ so unique in the **Bible** and distinguishes Him from every other person in human history, is His divinity. The term 'divinity' in the **Bible** has all to do with His divine nature. Christ in the **Bible** is both human and divine in that He has the spiritual nature of God and the physical nature of man. Just as God fashioned man's body from the ground found in the **Bible**, and breathed His spirit into him, the divine nature of God spoke Christ into existence within the womb of Mary. When you read the **Bible**, you will notice that Christ was so much like God, many did not look at Him as a man, and He was so much like man, He did not look like God. The **Bible** will only make complete sense to you if God breathes His divine nature into you. When you read the **Bible**, seek its revelation as well. Revelation does not come from human ingenuity, seminary, or any religious institutions; it is the sole work of the Holy Spirit of God found in the **Bible**. The principles in the inspirational book called the **Bible** can transform your life.

64 If you don't know the answer, don't make one up to save face.

No leader has the answers for everything, no matter how great he or she may be. However, there are some people who would want you to think they do. Making up an answer is the same as telling a lie. Many politicians, especially, know how to put their spin on words and would want you to think that they do have all the answers. Just listening to how some of these individuals rattle off answers to everything should tell you that they are making up answers as they go. How is it that two politicians can argue the same issue with answers diametrically in opposition to the other and both claiming to be right? I had a pastor friend of mine speak at a conference that I held in order to inspire our parishioners to become proactive in the public sphere. Here is what he said: "You know that some politician is lying when you see his lips moving." The vast majority of what politicians tell you about what they will do once elected is unlikely to happen simply because those decisions cannot be made by one person. It would be more practical for them to say what they will try and hope to do, but that type of language doesn't drive people to the voting booth. Making up answers and saying what people want to hear is how the game works. Never be afraid to say, "I don't know, but I will try to find the answer and get back to you." As Abraham Lincoln said, "You can fool some of the people all of the time, and all of the people some of the time, but you cannot fool all of the people all of the time."

65

A broken heart that has been healed has more capacity to love than one that has not.

"Therefore, I say unto you, her sins, which are many, are forgiven; for she loved much: but to whom little is forgiven, the same loves little." (Luke 7:47) In this passage, Jesus establishes why those who have had more challenges in their lives and have been healed are more likely to be sensitive to the pain of others, as opposed to those who haven't had as many misfortunes. It has been said that everyone's heart should be broken at least once. While I don't wish for a broken heart to happen to anyone, I do agree that a person whose heart has been healed from brokenness is generally more sensitive to the needs of others. Some of the greatest lessons that I learned in life were after my heart was broken. Heartbreak can come from death of a loved one, broken relationships or failure to accomplish certain goals. Whatever the cause might be, once you come to terms with your pain and allow God to heal your heart, you will be a better person. Pain should help teach you to trust God more, and to show humility, compassion and a greater capacity for love and sympathy when others are hurt. There is an ancient African proverb that states, "Never judge a man until you have walked a mile in his shoes." I have heard it said a thousand times, "If I were you I would do thus and so." People who make this statement oftentimes have to retract it once they have experienced a life-altering situation.

66

Not only do we reap what we sow, but we also reap what we haven't sown.

Sowing and reaping is a natural and spiritual universal law. Farmers plant year-round globally with exciting expectation of reaping the harvest that was sown months earlier. They don't just haphazardly expect anything to come up from the ground, but a harvest that is commensurate to the seeds that were sown. Relationally, the concept of sowing and reaping is no different. You can reasonably expect to enjoy the type of relationship that you are willing to work for with other people. The Bible teaches that those who wish to have friends must first be willing to show themselves friendly. If you sow the seeds of friendship, friends you will attract. However, there will be times when relational seeds will crop up that you have not sown. Sometimes, your enemy, Satan, will take the liberty to plant the seeds of discord against you in order to create a distraction in your life. He uses people who are already hurt or weak to sow the seeds of hurt in others. You may find yourself in a serious and contentious battle with someone that you had absolutely nothing to do with creating. It is tantamount to getting shot in a drive-by as an innocent bystander; it's called collateral damage. You reap the pain of another person's indiscretion, especially in a relationship where there are soul ties. Life does happen to us along this journey, and when it does, use it as an opportunity to grow and get closer to God. All suffering in the kingdom is redemptive; in all things give thanks unto God!

Dr. Edward Lee Johnson Sr.

67

Religion has more to do with man trying to reach God than with God reaching man.

Religion is perhaps the most divisive entity in all of history. The vast majority of humanity does believe in God in one form or another, but we worship that God in a million conflicting ways. For the Judeo-Christian faith, there are over 38,000 different factions. And this figure is conservative. As Christians, we believe that God sent His Son Jesus to atone for the sins of the world. Jesus combined all the Old Testament laws into two. So if we actually believe in Him, religion is irrelevant because He did away with it. If we love God with every fiber of our being, and love our neighbors as we love ourselves, that's the fulfilled life. Why would anyone want religion when the way to God is so simple? To choose religion rather than the relational covenants that we are called to live is tantamount to traveling the world on horses when you have access to a Lear jet. Whereas religion is a ritual in which man tries to appease God, covenants are principles that teach us how to have a relationship with Him. Man's religion is nothing more than his way of trying to manipulate God through works, and to appear as if he knows God in the eyes of men. God has absolutely no interest in man's religion; but what He does want is an honest heart that will live by His covenants. Here is what He thinks about religion: "I hate, I despise your feast days, and I will not smell in your solemn assemblies" (Amos 5:21-22). God wants judgment and righteousness on Earth, not religion.

68

An addiction to anything is a clear indication that there is a deficit in the soul; fill the void and the addiction will cease.

As a teenager I became so dependent on alcohol, marijuana, uppers and sedatives, I was almost addicted. Addiction is a persistent, compulsive dependence on a behavior or substance. Addiction, substance or emotional, is a clear indication that there is a spiritual deficit within the heart. The human spirit, a specimen of God within the physical body of man, is designed to be self-sufficient. Man in his original state is God in the flesh just like Christ. When Jesus came to Earth, His assignment was to bring restoration to the human spirit by reconnecting us to God. Obedience on our part to God through His WORD is the only way that this process can be completed. When the spirit and soul of man is corrupted by any other substance, he becomes dependent on other things and not God. Whether it's drugs, sex, alcohol, soul ties to other people and even food addictions; it's a clear indication that there is a breakdown in man's relationship with his Creator. Our sufficiency at all times should be rooted in the faith that we have in Christ. There is no lasting fulfillment of the soul of a man aside from the spirit of God. Reconnect with God's spirit and begin to free yourself from addictions. Thinking the right thoughts, associating with the right people and taking extra care of your physical health is the key to becoming fulfilled. If your spirit is free of toxic thinking, it gives you the power to control your appetite.

Dr. Edward Lee Johnson Sr.

69

Never allow your children to come between your relationship with your spouse.

Marriage was designed by God for the purpose of procreation and the establishment of a kingdom model on the Earth. God's relationship with His Son Christ is likened to the relationship between a man and his wife. Before the fall of Adam and Eve in the Garden there were no children, and they both had equal dominion. Mandatory submission of Eve to Adam was a part of the curse. Eve was not created to be dominated by Adam, and neither was she to suffer during childbirth. With the two of them having equal dominion, their relationship should have been one of mutual submission. This process would have been very simple because they were created to complete one another. Accommodating one another through love and respecting the gifting of each other is the perfect marriage. When children are birthed into a relationship, they should simply model the pattern that is seen in mother and father. Parents can only squelch disobedience in children when respect for each other is shared by both. The problems with the children are the parents. Children should never come between the relationship of husbands and wives. If spouses knew how to make each other a priority, children would love what they see and model it. Never argue with each other, especially in the presence of the children. Disagreement is common, but arguments are selfish. Make your spouse a priority at all times.

70 The family is the fundamental building block of society; if your family life is in order, chances are everything else in your life will fall in place.

Morality, spirituality, obedience, love, compassion, security, appreciation, character, tolerance, and respect are all relational principles that should be learned from good parents. All of these principles, or the lack thereof, is reflected in how an individual is raised; and, their willingness to adopt the right values. Just like good principles are learned, corrupt ones are learned as well. Race and racism would not be an issue if it was not being perpetuated by parents or other close associates. Statistics have proven this to be true across the board within every ethnic community. This is true primarily because the healthy relationship between the father and mother serves as a catalyst for producing healthy children. Healthy adults are simply healthy children who held on to the values that were taught to them in their formative years. Studies have proven that children aged six to ten years have permanently formed 90 percent of their values. (University of Washington News 2015) America and nations around the world would be better served if there was more awareness of this fact. If one percent of the monies wasted in governmental programs were used to promote healthy family values, our nation would be transformed in one generation. All of the good moral values that are practiced around the world can be traced back to the family covenant that God made with Abraham in Genesis 12. Families that live by these principles are blessed by God.

Dr. Edward Lee Johnson Sr.

71

If you need a person more than he or she needs you, you may be resented for it.

Relational beings are what we are, but no one wants to feel as if they are being pulled or used by others. If an individual refuses to become well rounded and self-sufficient, he or she will look to someone else to lean on. In being self-sufficient, I simply mean a person who has to mature to the point where he or she is happy and content within. With some slight variation, we all have the same access to the God who is able to make us sufficient in all things. Becoming your brother's keeper has to be demonstrated through godly character; it should not mean that your brother should have the right to require of you what he is fully capable of providing for himself. If there is a need, true brotherhood should compel one to assist the individual in need. However, don't allow yourself to become so dependent on others, or vice versa, that it hinders you from functioning without them. Unless you are physically or mentally disabled, you should never become a burden on another person. Learn the secret to accessing God's help like so many others do every day. I'm not suggesting that you should not feel pain if you lose a loved one, experience divorce or broken friendship; however, life must go on. The only Person you should need more than a spouse, friends, loved ones or associates is your God. If you have Him, He will move the hearts of the right people to help you. Don't become a burden on others; they may resent you for it. Every relationship should be mutually beneficial.

72

The first impression is usually a lasting impression; it does not have to be the defining impression.

Judging from some of my own experiences, I have learned not to draw conclusions about anyone that I meet for the very first time. Even though I may have my opinion about them, I do not come to conclusions; that's called prejudice. I've met many people over the years who, after meeting me for the second or third time around, thought of me differently. It is usually after we have spoken on a more personal note that the defense is dropped. I have been told that my looks are a bit threatening, but it's definitely not intentional. I do try to look in the mirror often and see myself as others may see me to make sure I project what I want people to believe about me. However, I will go out of my way to clarify myself if my actions are mistaken by others. It is in the nature of human beings to naturally protect their emotions. So, most people don't take a second look at things if the situation is uncomfortable the first time around. Don't make a conclusive judgment about a person until every means has been exhausted to build a relationship. Love at first sight is rare, and almost never lasts. Time and effort can often bring you into a productive relationship that normally doesn't happen instantly. The "code word" is relationships; and happy relationships may take a second, third, fourth and even fifth impression before finding their niche. Remember this, there was a time when people believed the earth was flat--the first impression.

Dr. Edward Lee Johnson Sr.

73

The greatest gift that you can give to a man is his freedom; however, he must be taught that freedom comes with responsibility.

One of greatest tragedies in the African American experience is that Emancipation did not bring with it sufficient education for freedom. However, most of the suffering in the Black communities today is not simply the lack of education, but discipline. Discipline and responsibility are inseparable requirements for a happy and productive life. These principles must be developed through strong and caring parenting and mentoring. If the proper amount of knowledge, love and discipline is not equally applied, the individual will generally self-destruct. An education tells you what to do, but knowledge teaches you how to do it. Have you ever met a person who was highly educated, but had no common sense? Once you have learned the importance of personal responsibility, you will have already learned common sense as well. Strong moral character that comes from a respected mentor is an invaluable lesson. This is why godly parenting is so important. If moral character is not instilled during the formative years of childhood, it will not automatically set in with old age. That is one main reason why young Black men are going to prison at epidemic proportions. The human spirit is so fragile that education in itself can be more destructive than good, if it is not accompanied with strong mentoring. Before a man is given his freedom, he should be given the tools needed to manage it.

74

There are only two premises from which every person develops his or her morals: evil or good.

In our modern era of political correctness, people generally have some trepidation about calling certain things evil. All good comes from God, all evil comes from the devil, and the Bible is where these premises are found. You may disagree with this principle, but as the author of this book, I happen to believe that the Bible is the foundation for all truth. The scriptures clearly delineate and lay the foundation for the Bible being the source from which we understand good and evil. There is no other book more ancient than the Bible that teaches the principle of good and evil. Those who consider themselves atheists, deists and agnostics all question the authenticity of God in the Bible. Giving deference to the opinion of others, I respect every person's right to be wrong who disagrees with me on the authenticity of the Bible; it's the noble thing to do. We would have a better world if people chose not to push their beliefs down the throats of others. I happen to know the Bible because of its incredible transformative effect on my life and all those who submit to its principles. When you take a closer look at its content, you will see the superior fingerprint of a supreme God in its narratives. I do agree that it was written by man, but it's the revelation of God. No human is capable of raising himself from infancy to adulthood. So, if the first man was a god, there had to have been a greater God that raised him. The greater one is the God of the Bible; He is the source of all good things.

Dr. Edward Lee Johnson Sr.

75

No matter how strong your belief system in life may be, always leave room for God to change your mind.

Your belief system is the ideology you develop over time as a result of upbringing, exposure and influences. You are literally what you think: "Whatever a man thinks of himself, that's who he really is." (Proverbs 23:7) Our beliefs are strengthened or weakened based on what we continue to expose ourselves to. The longer we hold to our beliefs, the harder it becomes to depart from them. In the book of Jonah the story is told of how Jonah tried to avoid a missionary journey that God instructed him to carry out. He was sent to Nineveh to preach a revival, but Jonah did not take kindly to this nation because they were once enemies of Israel. Jonah had taken issue with God and decided to abort his mission, only to be swallowed by a fish for three days. The Apostle Peter was faced with a similar mission when, as recorded in Acts 10, he was told through a vision to go and minister to a gentile family. Both men at first refused, but then reluctantly heeded God's call to preach to their non-Jewish neighbors, even though they were servants of God. The story is told of a drowning man who prayed for God's help to keep him from drowning. A boat, helicopter and a ocean liner stopped to help him, but he refused them all, stating that God would send him help. Well, he drowned and went to heaven. "Why did you let me drown he asked God?" God replied, "I sent you help but you refused it." You may be sincere in your beliefs, but you can be sincerely wrong.

76

Positive, goal-oriented people are generally happier because it helps them to fantasize throughout life.

If you aim at nothing you will surely hit it. By the time we reach adolescence, we should have begun to think strongly of what we hope to become as full-fledged adults. Here are just a few positive goals to think about: the way you intend to practice your faith in God, i.e. faith affiliation, the career you hope to establish, what you hope for in your potential mate and spouse whether you should remain single, your financial portfolio and even the city you plan to settle in are some fundamental goals that everyone should have. Have you ever noticed how carefree a child is when he or she has the freedom to fantasize about life? A child's fantasy should be a model for the way adults set goals; you're simply dreaming of what you would like to become. Reaching for things that are beyond your sight is literally an act of faith. The reason why faith is such a positive thing is because it gives you something that you don't actually have. When you set goals, you are literally trusting God to give you something that you don't currently have. A child's imaginary friend, money, and ability are God-given gifts that assist the child in growing up. The restriction of the imagination is the most crippling thing that can be done to a child. If you must interfere with a child's fantasy, assist him in imagining something that is more positive than what he is fantasizing at the moment. Set positive goals, believe that you can achieve them by the help of God, and you will never have a dull moment in life even if you don't reach them all.

Dr. Edward Lee Johnson Sr.

77

Never usurp authority over people, but see yourself as a facilitator who helps others achieve as well as yourself.

The human spirit was created to be self-governed, people who do not really understand this fact allow themselves to be subjugated and dominated by others. Although there are many people who are quite challenged when it comes to staying focused and becoming great achievers, see yourself as the person who is there to help others excel in life. Never forget that people do not follow you simply because of who you are, but because of what you do for them. That is why so many people resort to manipulation and corruption in order to keep themselves in power. Helping others to achieve is the heart of a great leader. King David united the fledgling tribes of Israel and brought them to great standing alongside the other tribal nations in that region. He knew how to motivate his men and encouraged them to work together because they wanted to, and not just because of him. Jonathan was the son of a king and David was a king in the making, but the two of them never sought to dominate one another, but became soul mates for the kingdom. David was obviously very good at this because Jonathan, as a prince, gave up his desire to become king and pushed David to the forefront. Nehemiah was another great motivator: he went back to Jerusalem and rallied a team of fellow Israelites to rebuild the wall around the city in 52 days. Help others, and they will help you to achieve your goals. Lead by influence and people will gravitate toward you.

78

It is impossible to develop people skills without interacting with them.

The term "skill" is defined as "the ability to effectively accomplish a task with little energy or effort." A person who goes to class for two hours without taking notes on the material discussed in class and aces the test has learning skills. A basketball player who repeatedly assists in winning the game and scores an average of 30 points a game has skills. A pastor who can keep a congregation happy for more than 25 years has skills. Politicians who can get themselves voted into office at the end of every term have skills; you get the point. All of the previous statements are true because the individuals develop their skills and put them to work. As a leader, if you expect to win the support of people to accomplish your goals, you must develop people skills. When you begin to interact with people, you learn their habits, as well as their social, physiological and spiritual make up. Your association with people is how you develop people skills. The desire to be loved, to gain knowledge, to be respected and to provide for oneself are universal human quests. Use these tips to develop your skills as a leader of people, and they will endear themselves to you for life. I do not suggest that you become this type of individual, but even if you don't love people, your skills in human relations can influence them to rally to your cause. People don't care how much you know, until they know how much you care. Even if you don't care, if they believe you do, it will work as well.

Dr. Edward Lee Johnson Sr.

79

Learning to become disciplined can be your greatest achievement in life.

Disciplined people put their goals in life above all else. Nelson Mandela, the first black president of South Africa, spent thirty years in jail before he achieved his ultimate goal. What do you think would have become of him had he not disciplined himself for the vision that was within him. If you study the term discipline, you will learn that it comes from the word disciple, which are the Latin word for pupil. The disciples of Jesus were able to transform the world because they disciplined themselves by the principles that He taught during the three and a half years that He ministered on Earth. Discipline in your spiritual devotion, thoughts, social habits, work ethics, eating habits, relationships, time, and education are the foundation for a happy and fulfilled life. I consider myself to be a conservative, and my wife a liberal, but we balance one another in order to raise happy and healthy children. I am not mean-spirited as a conservative and neither is she morally corrupt as a liberal. True love comes together in order to accomplish what neither individual can do alone. Poverty, the worst of human disorders, can be overcome if a person is willing to simply restrain themselves from certain pleasures. I don't necessarily like the terms conservative and liberal simply because they have become divisive talking points for politicians and talk show hosts. You can be disciplined on either side if you really understand the terms. As a teenager I was extremely undisciplined, but I decided to grow up.

80 Always respect the time of other people; if you abuse it, you may not get it again.

Oftentimes I have been invited to events or have scheduled appointments with people only to have my time wasted by someone who was unorganized, or just did not respect me enough to manage the time. How does it make you feel when you have been invited to a place or have a scheduled appointment and you have to wait thirty minutes to an hour for the other party? If I request a forum with an individual I especially make it a practice to be ahead of time. Being punctual and honoring the time of others says to them that you respect them and their time as well. If you plan an event and invite others to come, be mindful that people are doing you a favor by attending. Never become so self-absorbed that you begin to think that the world revolves around you. If you are good at something, chances are there is someone else who is just as good or better at it than you are. You should use money and love people. However, there are a lot of people who have gotten this concept twisted. They use people and love money. Having access to the time of others should be considered an honor; don't abuse it. If there comes a time when you request the time of someone else, and that particular time cannot be honored, give the person ample notice to adjust his or her schedule as well. In doing so, he or she will probably have a more favorable opinion of you for doing so. As a professional, respecting other people can be your greatest asset; use their time wisely.

Dr. Edward Lee Johnson Sr.

81 Eternity is too long to get it wrong.

If you spent one thousand years on this earth and discovered that there is no hell, that would be great. However, if you spent one million years on Earth and found that there is, it would be a tragedy. Illustration: If you took a teaspoon and begin to empty all the world's oceans, seas, rivers, lakes, ponds, ditches, and puddles, it would only be equivalent to a split second in eternity. We view time as linear but God's time is cyclical. In essence, there is no end to time; Man's time continues in cycle. If there is any doubt in your mind as to the truth about this subject, don't wait until your time is up here on Earth to find the truth. There are too many books you can read, people you can see, and places you can go to find out the truth on the subject. In my sharing with people about their relationship with God, I sometimes get the feeling that they believe God is hard-up to save them. Human beings were created to make choices of their own free will, and God Himself will not violate our will. God is not going to force Himself on us. He has rolled out the red carpet for humanity to find the answer to the hard questions about eternity. The red carpet is literally dyed with the red blood of His Son, the truth is so easy to find a child can lead you to it, the way is so clear you don't need to carry a light, the path is so straight you don't have to turn, there is only one door you don't have to guess, and the price is free so you don't have to pay to receive it; and if after all of this and you still get it wrong, eternity is too long.

82 Diligence versus laziness or education versus ignorance, which do you think costs the most?

It was Benjamin Franklin who coined this phrase: "If you think education is expensive, try ignorance." In the short run, it will cost absolutely nothing for you to be lazy and ignorant to the things that matter most to your wellbeing. However, in the long-run it will cost you everything as your progeny will begin to spiral to the lowest level of the economic strata. If you live long enough, you will see those who have been influenced by slothfulness and ignorance fill the prisons and suffer disproportionately with health issues. Some people will go to work and find a million ways to get by with doing as little as possible while someone else on the same job will look for ways to help the company prosper. Having worked in the construction business for a great portion of my life, I have watched some guys who refuse to go to work even when a vehicle was sent to pick them up from their front door. It's unfortunate, but you can have two individuals birthed from the same womb, raised by the same parents and one become rich and the other choose poverty. Laziness and ignorance is a curse, but it's also a decision. If you want to prosper and win in life, you must decide to develop a positive attitude, strong work ethics and begin to embrace achievers; success is contagious. An education may cost you more in the short run, but if you put the skills you learn to work, it would cost substantially less in the long run than the price of ignorance and laziness.

Dr. Edward Lee Johnson Sr.

83

You may have pulled yourself up by your own bootstraps, but don't forget someone designed the boot.

There is nothing more agitating than a snob. "A snob is a person with an exaggerated opinion of himself who believes that his tastes in a particular area are superior to those of other people." They are people who think the world revolves around them and want to take all the credit for everything they have accomplished. Everything that the snob accomplished is solely for the purpose of getting attention or proving a point. He is incapable of achieving real happiness because he can never be satisfied with what he has or has become. Pride, arrogance and selfishness are the core traits of a snob. It's like having an addiction: the more one has, the more one wants. The perfect candidates for this type of personality are those who have quickly forgotten what got them to where they are in life. You can be impoverished and still be a snob, but more often it's the person who has either received or has been exposed to a reasonable amount of success. Never refuse to acknowledge that someone else is partly responsible for your success. Successful people have to their credit someone who believed in them, or believed in what they pursued and accomplished. I have known people who worked together for years and could not stand each other's guts, but they pursued together and accomplished what neither of them could have done on their own. Pulling yourself up by your bootstraps is good, but don't forget where the boot came from.

84

A title does not make you a leader any more than sitting in the cockpit of an aircraft makes you a pilot.

A title says you have the name, but your experience and relationships with people says you have the capability. I have been in the church all of my life and in ministry for nearly forty years, and one of the things that I have vividly noticed is that every man that can preach is not a pastor. And likewise, every great pastor is not a "gifted" preacher. Never become hung up on a title; it's only a label. The wise man Solomon said, "Your gift will make room for you…" If you have been duly trained and gifted to accomplish a task, your work will speak for you, and your influence with people is what makes you a leader and not a title. Becoming bent out of shape and hung up on a title has more to do with vanity than substance. If you are capable of moving an agenda forward and commanding teamwork without driving yourself or the crowd, a leader you are. One of the great things about leadership is, if you are a leader, someone else besides you will know that you are. A man who says he is a leader without a following is a man taking a walk. The most important thing you can do if you have the aspiration for leadership is to polish up your act and master your craft, whatever that might be. Do what you do with such skill, vigor, precision and accuracy, that people will show to watch you burn even if you don't have a title. If someone chooses not to respect you or the position you hold, it's their problem not yours. Use a towel to serve, not your title to intimidate.

Dr. Edward Lee Johnson Sr.

85

The attitude you reveal is the attitude you attract.

The single most contributing factor to a happy and productive life is your attitude. A noted author and motivational speaker by the name of Charles R. Swindall said, "Attitude is more important than fact, money, education failure, circumstances, giftedness, skill or even what people say about you...." You are the most important factor to your future. Thousands of people will probably be enamored by you, but the ones that you will be with in a productive relationship are the ones that sincerely believe in you. In life, we actually produce after our kind. In essence, we speak what we know, but we reproduce who we are. If you are not happy with the type of people that you are attracting, you need to change, but do not blame the other person. It is imperative that you love who and what you have become, because you will have a lifetime to deal with you. People are not thinking about us nearly as much as we think they are. Sometimes they are overwhelmed with their own issues. There are signals (attitude) that radiate from every human being, and these signals can be picked up others. Your attitude frequency will draw to you those who are more like you. If you hope to attract vibrant, effervescent, productive, and exhilarating people in your life, develop these traits in your life. Everyone loves a winner, and it takes a winning attitude to become a winner in the marketplace of ideas. If you have the right attitude, the wrong people will refuse to stay connected to you.

86

Never get in a rush to do anything unless it is a desperate attempt to save your soul.

The tortoise and hare: The story is told of how the tortoise, a very slow moving creature, won the race against the hare, a creature that was fifty times faster in speed. In our modern culture of electronics, computers, supersonic aircrafts and even microwave ovens, we still don't seem to be satisfied with the rate of speed at which things are done. People are in such a vicious rat race trying to get more things that they cannot afford, with money they don't have, to impress people that they don't like. How sad is this? Forty years ago the only way most people could communicate from a distance was via a home or business telephone. Shortly afterward pagers became popular but we still had to wait or travel a distance to return a call. The bag cell phones hit the market shortly after the pager, but it was too embarrassing to carry around, so we left it in the car. Then the streamline car phones lasted for a brief period before the hand-held became popular. Before the 60s we had to wait as much as two weeks to receive mail depending upon where it was sent. The prolific use of the internet started in the 80s. Now, we can sit in front of a computer and receive mail from around the globe and we will get angry if the mail does not come through within seconds. We rush to wash-up, rush to get dressed, rush to eat and rush to work only to spend all day angry at a job that we don't like. With all this lightning speed many people are still not happy with life because all of what they treasured most has no lasting or intrinsic value.

Dr. Edward Lee Johnson Sr.

87

Everyone is motivated, or have the lack of motivation, depending upon how they feel.

If a person will tell me how she is feeling, I can probably tell her what she is thinking; your emotional and physical health is directly tied to your spiritual health. The way you think affects the way you feel, and the way you feel, affects the way you think; it's called psychosomatic. If you allow yourself to think about too many negative things or unresolved issues for too long, it will begin to affect you physically. It can produce headaches, stomach pain and even mimic a heart attack. A pressure cooker has a vent at the top in order to let off steam during the cooking process. Without the vent, steam from the condensation would blow the top off the pot. Your body works quite similarly. It is imperative that you guard your health because all of your productive days are dependent upon it. People who struggle everyday with getting out of bed and being productive in life are not normal. When your spirit is charged, it will trigger the energy that's needed for your body to produce. Little more than a decade ago I was building our dream home; during this time I came down with the flu that kept me in the bed for five days. After slightly recovering I was driving to a funeral that was near the house. When I got to the actual street that the house was on, I literally refused to look in that direction because I was physically and emotionally depleted. You should be full of enthusiasm, vitality and vigor as you rise every day to take dominion in your Heavenly Father's vineyard.

88

Time alone with God may not do anything for Him, but it is invaluable time for you.

Spending time alone with God achieves intimacy, something that no functioning relationship can do without. When Jesus said "depart from Me I never knew you," He meant intimacy. The term "knew" in scripture was used when Adam became intimate with Eve and produced their children. Quality time with God through meditation, prayer, study of the scriptures and occasional fasting are the fundamentals for spiritual intimacy. You should never have to find time to be alone with God, you should have a set time to be alone with Him. It should be as routine as eating and sleeping. Never get the idea that you are doing God a favor by setting yourself apart unto Him. Intimacy has everything to do with you allowing God to condition your heart so that He can prepare you to be used for His Kingdom. Whenever we become preoccupied with just business as usual and have no quality time with God, life becomes nothing more than a grinding routine. Life for the believer should be filled with excitement and adventure as the Holy Spirit leads us through each day. Never consider intimacy to be an inconvenience to you. It may sometimes feel that way, because in many ways our attitude towards God is no different from children towards parents; they want everything given to them but they do not want to earn it by doing things in return. Practice exercising intimacy with God each day and I promise you that life will never be the same as His peace settles in your heart.

Dr. Edward Lee Johnson Sr.

89

Always leave room for offence, and when it comes be quick to forgive.

The act of forgiveness is the fundamental principle of biblical Christianity; it was the only reason Jesus had to be sacrificed. "For God so loved the world that He gave His Son..." God gave His Son Christ, in order to make atonement for fallen humanity. His sacrifice made it possible for our sins to be forgiven, and forgiving others is one of the prerequisites for our sins to be forgiven. We must reconcile to God through His Son. Once the relationship was broken between God and man, mankind never properly learned how to relate one to another. The Bible is a simple message of relationships, either between God and man or between man and man. Relationships are built on covenants (agreement between parties) that teaches us how to relate to our fellowman. Satan, the arch enemy of God, would like to keep humanity in bondage and unforgiveness. When you choose not to forgive, you are allowing negative forces to manipulate your life. He will try to make you believe that holding on to issues against others somehow affects them, but you hurt the most when harboring bitterness and unforgiveness. Christ's suffering and death is in vain as far as you are concerned if you are not free from the bondage of unforgiveness and sin. Think of it this way, you cannot hold a person down without being held down as well. When you forgive others, you become free.

90

Be polite and courteous at all times and to everyone; you will reap the reward eventually.

Being polite to everyone you meet is one of the hallmarks of the Christian faith. I don't want to be mistreated, and it is unimaginable to me to purposely mistreat someone else; yet I see it happening every day. The entire world would be transformed in one day if this golden rule were practiced by everyone. "Do to others as you would like them to do to you." There are many depraved individuals in this world who are incapable of understanding this message, and there are millions of others who are good but insensitive to others. If we would just slow the pace down as we meander through this life, and look other people in the eyes as we meet them, the process of being courteous can start immediately. If we literally begin to look at other people as if they are a part of us, we will treat them differently. After all, all of us did come from one flesh. We eat the same food, breathe the same air, bleed red blood and hope to be in a meaningful relationship with someone. So, why can't we all get along? We are all selfish in one way or another and therefore must work a little harder in our relationships towards others. The more we work on our spirituality and become more intimate with our Creator, He will teach us how to become more sensitive and affectionate. The fruit of the spirit is love, joy, peace, faith, meekness, kindness, goodness, temperance, and longsuffering. These attributes are the characteristics of Christ, and His followers should allow them to be displayed in their lives with everyone they meet.

Dr. Edward Lee Johnson Sr.

91

Influence is the greatest weapon against rejection; use it to reach a person's heart instead of your ability to control him or her.

The word influence is literally defined as "to flow into." Think of a clear glass vessel that is either filled with fluid, or void of it. To the extent that the glass is filled, it has more fluid within. On the other hand, if it is near empty, it has less fluid within. Compare the fluid within a glass to a relationship: the more a person believes in, respects and looks up to you, the more he or she is influenced by you. As a leader, you will get more out of an individual when he or she is influenced by you. As humans, we are relational beings; and even if a person knows of you only from a distance, his perception is his reality. If he feels good about you, chances are you can influence him to see things your way. Unless you are an officer of the law, and someone is in violation of it, you cannot make him or her listen or follow you. On the other hand, if you have influence "fluid in," you can get someone to do basically what you want of her own volition by simply asking. Hopefully the analogy is very clear to you at this point; so begin to develop some new strategies and people skills in order to accomplish the vision, goal and dreams that you have been gifted with. If people are driven by your authority alone, they will resent you. Of course, some people will not follow you if you paid them to because they do not like you; in such a case, move on to the ones who want to hear what you have to offer.

92

Refusing to confront an issue will make it go away, but only for the moment.

You cannot conquer what you refuse to confront, and you will not confront what you will not admit. Some people are masters of disguise. You can look at them and they seem to be sitting on top of the world, but the moment you begin to converse with them, their words reveal a different story. We learn very early in life to compartmentalize our lives. Some people have a home life, church life, on the job life and a night life. We reveal a different side of ourselves in each environment because we learn how to do whatever it takes for us to get by. We do, act and say one thing when we are with certain people; then we change when we are in another setting. Emotional trauma, sexual abuse, neglect and insecurity are only a few reasons why people portray such vacillating dispositions. We refuse to become transparent because it's too painful; so we live double lives. The only way to stabilize this type of temperament is to confront the issues in your life. Come to terms with the challenges you are facing and trust God to connect you with someone who can support you through your struggles. Not everyone is out to get you, but there are some people that have been gifted by God just to help you. If you are willing to confront your issues, God will empower you to conquer them. Admit it, confront it and conquer it with the help of God and some trusted friends. In fact, you have my permission to email me and I will steer you in the right direction in order to see you happy; this is what I do.

Dr. Edward Lee Johnson Sr.

93

One quote from the Bible can create a world-wide utopia.

Christ taught these words while here on Earth, "Thou shalt love the Lord thy God with all thy heart, and with all thy soul, and with all thy strength, and with all thy mind; and thy neighbour as thyself." If this single commandment were adhered to by everyone, here is what you could expect in the world:

- All houses of worship filled to capacity
- No alarm systems, locks or protector guards
- No murders, physical or verbal abuse
- No child molestation, abuse or trafficking
- No rape, sodomy or same-sex marriages
- No fear, fighting or physical abuse
- No lying, cheating or backbiting
- No road rage, outrage, or grandstanding
- No divorce, abortions or dead-beat dads
- No racial strife, class envy or wealth disparity
- No theft, coveting or jealousy
- No wars, empire building or gated communities
- No poverty, hunger, homelessness or nakedness
- No penal institutions, or houses of prostitution
- No worship of any God but Jehovah
- Did I miss something? Write it here _____

WOW, what a wonderful world this would be!

94

What you do from a pure heart to help someone else may go unnoticed, but it will not go unrewarded.

#When you give something to a needy person, do not make a big show of it, as the hypocrites do in the houses of worship and on the streets. They do it so that people will praise them. I assure you, they have already been paid in full. But when you help a needy person, do it in such a way that even your closest friend will not know about it. Then it will be a private matter. And your Father, who sees what you do in private, will reward you." (GNT) This passage serves to underscore just how much value God places on the service we render to Him, as well as what we do on behalf of our fellowman. Since our faith and commitment to service is unto an unseen God, we are challenged here in scripture to validate our loyalty to Him by serving without the need to be seen by man. Our entire reward for the work that is done on Earth will be judged by what we did from a pure heart as a result of our faith in God, and not the quantity of our gifts. What we do on earth on His behalf for the least of men should be done as if we were actually doing it unto the Lord. Many on the final Day of Judgment will try to get into His kingdom on their works alone, but they will be sadly disappointed to hear the Lord say, depart from me because all that you did on earth was done for self-promotion. Faith is the only work that God honors, so don't be weary in well doing, you will reap a great reward. You will be rewarded as long as God gets the glory and it does not matter to you who gets the credit.

Dr. Edward Lee Johnson Sr.

95 There is such a thing as becoming too humble; it's when you are proud of it.

There are some people who try to portray a disposition of humility, but it's nothing more than puritanical and self-righteousness. Before I make the attempt to define what humility is, let me first of all say what it is not: it is not looking pitiful, feeling sorry for yourself, acting pious, ignorant, being impoverished, or feeling the need to be needed. Humility is the careful commitment not to think of yourself as more than who you are or what you have become. It is an instant readiness to submit to the direction and correction of God, man, and even a child if needed. It is an act of service rendered for the benefit of mankind on God's behalf and not our own. When you are truly humble, there is a grace that emanates from you; others will perceive and receive of the qualities you possess. When you pretend to be something that you are not, someone will always pick up on your insincerity. You can fool some of the people some of the time, and all of the people some of the time, but you cannot fool all the people all the time. Humility is simply honesty and the excellence of character. The Pharisees were masterful actors in their attempt to outwardly convince others that they were godly and humble, but their ulterior motive was to be seen as people of importance (pride). They embellished themselves in the finest of garments, and were highly visible in the marketplace seeking the attention of men. They that know God will be humble; they that know themselves cannot be proud.

96

Anger, even when justified, should always be directed towards helping an individual, and not destroying him or her.

The first human response to anger is generally to inflict some type of emotional or bodily harm to the individual who caused the pain. Evil does not have a face; however, it uses all types of faces to accomplish its goals. Inflicting bodily punishment to an individual should only be done for one purpose, and that is to motivate him to do good. If it is done for any other reason, it simply perpetuates anger. I have raised 6 children of my own, and I did not do a lot of spanking, but I do have a tendency to yell. They have learned that I elevate my voice as a last resort before spanking. When I did spank, it was never out of anger, but out of a heart of love in order to correct them. "We wrestle not against flesh and blood but against powers, principalities and spiritual wickedness in high places." (Ephesians 6:13) When you become angry with a person for the purpose of being malicious, it proves your ignorance of the real enemy, Satan. Satan influences every evil act that is committed by human beings. So, if you must fight, and you must, let it be the good fight against evil, and not the individual. Evil does not have a face; it's a force. When you learn to fight evil successfully, you will always leave room for the person that is influenced by the force of evil to change. Life is about good and evil; good people are influenced by God and evil people by the devil (God good--devil evil). Harboring anger against a person is always misdirected.

Dr. Edward Lee Johnson Sr.

97

What you refuse to master will eventually master you.

The story is told in a novel *Frankenstein* by Mary Shelley how Victor Frankenstein created a monster which eventually murdered members of Victor's family, and because Victor could not satisfy him, he plotted to take Victor's life as well. This classic work of fiction ironically depicts in some ways what we have become as a human race, even with the advancement of masterful scientific technologies. We have mastered the sophisticated crafts of automobiles, airplanes, television, computers, telephones, military weapons of war and have even landed a man on the moon. However, never before in the history of humanity have we had the capability to annihilate the human race from the face of the planet with the touch of a few buttons. Even with these technologies, we have yet to learn how to master the human spirit. Consequently, mankind is consumed with the use of legal and illicit drugs, alcohol, sexual promiscuity, sleep deprivation, violence, and the dissolution of family values. Millions live in utter fear each day wondering what might become of them as the day passes on. We can travel the world from our living room on the "world wide web," but our relationships and willingness to trust one another is eroding all the more. We have literally become the monster that we must save ourselves from. Until the human heart is mastered by his maker, no amount of human effort can stop the downward spiral of moral decadence.

98

Personal responsibility is the highest order in life.

People who refuse to accept responsibility by blaming another for their actions are: childish, an imbecile, irrational, selfish, foolish, ignorant, or simply willfully defiant. The very first mistake that Adam made was to blame Eve for something he was told not to do. Likewise, Eve sought to blame the serpent for her disobedience. Cain, their son, on the other hand, did not blame anyone for his half-hearted offering but he was just nonchalant. Every action of an individual can be judged from a position of responsibility or irresponsibility. You were created to be self-governed, and the moment you refuse to manage your own affairs, you immediately give someone else that power over your life. It is your choice to surrender control but you should not complain when things don't go your way; it's the price paid for being irresponsible. If you did it, said it, or neglected it, own up to it. If it turned out well, take the credit, if it turned out bad, take the blame. Your health, education, financial wellbeing, and relationships are solely your responsibility. If you are unhappy in any area of your life, you can correct it by starting with the man in the mirror. Most people are willing to help, but not at their expense. Health care is not a right but a privilege. Doctors who practice medicine do so at their pleasure, and those who seek their services should do so with this in mind. Teaching others to properly manage their health should be the first priority for those who seek to promote national health care. If not, it may frustrate the grace of the professionals who can refuse to practice medicine.

Dr. Edward Lee Johnson Sr.

99

The first command is to love the Lord with all your heart, the second is to love your neighbor as yourself, and the third is, Just do it.

What the world needs more of is money, right? Wrong answer—it's love. All the money in this world cannot buy love, or teach you how to love. Love is defined in different ways, depending on who you ask. In most cases, it is defined by our feelings, which is not love at all. If what you feel is the right feeling, it is the result of love. Love is like a nerve, which does not feel, but it is what makes you feel. Love is what you do; it's an action. As a result of the right actions, it stimulates our emotions, which is how we feel love. When a person is fully developed in love, people to them become nameless and faceless, and they love in spite of, not because of. They relate to people according to their spirit and not their physical appearance. Love does not hold a grudge, nor will it stand in the way of your success. Love does not hold the past against you if you are willing to start right today. Love does not seek validation from others. True love is a state of being, and not a state of mind. Your mind changes at the drop of a hat, but that would not change who you are if you really have love. A person who loves literally wishes the best for all, and not just those who cater to him. The individual who loves effectively will not impose his will on others; however, he would attempt to persuade others in his direction. In case you want to know W.W.J.D. when it comes to loving other people, I just told you, "just do it."

100 What a noticeable difference one man can make!

Having familiarized myself somewhat with history, it has become clear to me that every major event in history was influenced by one man initially. Great Empires of antiquity, Middle Ages, and the modern era have all spiraled into greatness by the leadership of one man. Sumer, Egypt, Israel, Assyria, Babylon, Persia, Greece, Rome, the Ottoman Empire and Europe have all sprung to greatness by the leadership of one man. Although the United States is not considered an Empire, it exercises the same, if not a greater influence upon world affairs just like the great empires of the past. Individuals like Nimrod, Abraham, Hammurabi, Rameses II, Moses, Tiglath-Pileser I, Nebuchadnezzar II, Cyrus, Alexander the Great, Julius Caesar, Christ (the greatest), Muhammad, Genghis Khan, Hitler, Martin Luther, Abraham Lincoln, and Martin Luther King Jr., all made an indelible impression upon the world. When you add to this list the host of military generals, entrepreneurs, doctors and physicians, entertainers and educators, one man or woman usually sticks out among this list in history. You too, as one man or woman can make a noticeable impact in life even if it's not on a grand scale like some of the ones I have listed. You simply need to use all of your God-given talents, build strong relationships with like-minded individuals and be tenacious in your pursuit. Do it for God's glory and not self-aggrandizement and you will become a force for good that will inspire others to achieve greatness as well.

BONUS Principle You cannot make another person happy; happiness is a gift, one must choose it.

You may be able to make people laugh, but if they are to truly be happy, there are universal laws that must be followed. Laughter is only a temporary emotion but happiness is a state of mind. Too often people will blame others for their unhappiness but unhappiness is really a choice. People are unhappy and lonely in most cases because they build walls and not bridges. True happiness is the result of positive decisions made by individuals as it relates to their Creator, themselves and those with whom they are closely associated. Your moral values, based on fundamental Biblical and spiritual truths are the surest way to lasting happiness. Although there are people who may not be closely connected to any Biblical or religious influences directly, having known or been in relationships with people who live by Biblical principles can have positive effects on their lives. It is the decisions that you make from day to day, the position and disposition that you take on specific issues that will help to determine your happiness. If you can keep your heart clear of unforgiveness, bitterness, envy, strife and jealousy towards others, happiness will rest in your heart. Of course, this is provided you have established a social life with like-minded people; happiness is contagious. If you are standing in a crowded room and everyone breaks out laughing, you will probably begin to laugh simply because of the euphoria in the room. Associate with happy people and it will spread to you as well.

Conclusion

The principles in this book are practiced around the world by everyone who enjoys meaningful relationships. If you decide from this day forward to use these wisdom keys, doors will begin to open that would otherwise be impossible for you. More importantly, you will find peace, happiness and fulfillment as you embrace the "Life Skill" tips. The only place you should want to go in life is where God is leading you. The only people that you should establish relationships with are those who share your dreams and passions. The only people that you should seek to get even with are those that have helped you.

True character is defined by what you would do if no one could find out what you did. Integrity and character are the only way anyone can live up to the qualities that I describe and prescribe in this book. Integrity and character go together like wet and water; they are one and the same. People of character and integrity will swear to their own hurt before they refuse to honor their word. Once you have come to terms with the consequences of your actions, and are disciplined enough to hold yourself accountable, you have won the battle of integrity. People who struggle with deep character flaws are usually not so ready and willing to pull out all of the skeletons from the closet in order to be happy and develop good characteristics. Somehow, they have convinced themselves that if they come totally clean on the inside, they may miss out on some future desired pleasure, or perhaps people may not like them if their secrets were out in the open. The word integrity literally means to become at-one with oneself. Think of the word grid, or interlock. When your soul (emotions) is interlocked with your spirit, quality characteristics are produced. When this truly happens, you lose all desire to do anything that is untoward, sinister or evil. There are such things as soul ties and other emotional attachments that we sometimes have to battle with. Being connected to the wrong things or the wrong people can be a challenge to break away from; however, you're the captain of your own ship, so don't sink it.

God designed this world to build His Kingdom. However, Satan has set out to abort this plan. However, he is in for a rude awakening because the gates of hell cannot prevail against God's kingdom. What Adam failed to establish in Genesis 2 & 3, was given to Abraham in Genesis 12, 2000 years later. Christ completed what Abraham started 2000 years before His birth, and now, 2000 years after Christ, the Kingdom has come. After twelve centuries of religious dominance in the Western world, Martin Luther, a German monk, wrote his 95 Theses and pinned it to the Wittenberg Castle door in protest of the dogma that existed within the church during that time. Disgruntled followers defecting from the church in masses prompted the Reformation Movement from the 14th to the 16th centuries. This movement gave way to an expression of denominational factions by the thousands; over 38,000 from what I last read in the statistics of Christian denominations. Now it's time for another paradigm, the Kingdom of God manifested on Earth. As the apostolic and prophetic voices are synergized in this new era, there will be a productive working relationship achieved among the spiritual institutions within their cities. Then, the kingdoms of this world would become the kingdoms of our Lord, and of His Christ. Leaders, emerging leaders and world leaders will do well to align themselves with the plan of God or find themselves on the wrong side of history.

Eve's mandatory submission to Adam in the Garden of Eden was because of the curse after the fall of man. Prior to the fall, there was equal submission between them. They were spiritually designed to be mutually submitted to one another through love and respect. Just like it takes protons, electrons and neutrons to produce an atom, it takes a spiritually healthy father, mother and children to produce a kingdom model of the family. The curse of Adam's ruling over Eve was broken as a result of Christ conquering sin. The only way a man can justify ruling his wife under the New Covenant would be to remain under that curse. The restoration of marriage through kingdom principles is God's true order in the Earth. Through happy marriage relationships godly principles are taught and caught. As the principles are passed on and modeled by children, healthy children produce happy families, and happy families is the only method for transforming society. It is only through the spiritual principles of marriage that stable homes, stable communities, and stable nations are built. Anything short of mutual love and respect for our fellow man will continue to breed resentment, strife, envy and hatred for one another.

References

What I have shared in this book are deeply rooted principles that were sown into my life from childhood and cultivated over a generation. The Holy Bible is by far my greatest inspiration and that's the reason why it has been referenced throughout this book. The other references that are used come from books, relationship experiences and a wealth of other resource materials that I have studied throughout my life. This life-skill handbook should be kept close by at all times as a reference guide to some of the challenges you are sure to encounter from day to day.

May goodness, mercy, grace, and peace follow you all the days of your life.

Printed in the United States
by Baker & Taylor Publisher Services